The Pinch of the Crab and other stories

Barbara Southard

Copyright©2023
The Pinch of the Crab and other stories
©Barbara Southard
Crab and Tinglar Publishing
ISBN 978-1-64704-724-5
All rights reserved.

Author: Barbara Southard
Cover Design: Shaila Malia Choudhury Madero

Originally published in San Juan, Puerto Rico USA in 2021 by Publicaciones Puertorriquenas, Inc.
www.ppeditores.com

Several of the stories in this collection have appeared elsewhere. "Heavy Downpour" was published in the online journal *Calabash*. Slightly different versions of "The Pinch of the Crab," "Neighbors," and "Internal Injuries," were published in *Poui: Cave Hill Journal of Creative Writing*. A longer version of "En el campo" appeared in *The Journal of Caribbean Literatures*.

This collection of short stories is sponsored by:

Moonwired/Amanecidas:
Literary Review of the Women's
Bilingual Collective of Puerto Rico/
Revista literaria de la colectiva
bilingüe de escritoras de Puerto Rico
(www.moonwired.org)

Praise for
The Pinch of the Crab

"In these stories, universal themes in literature grip readers like a vise. The author depicts the external calamities of the Tropics in an uneasy alliance with internal worlds struggling to make sense of life. Reader beware: these characters will trigger emotions in you so complex you didn't know you were capable of experiencing them."

—María Soledad Rodríguez

"The Pinch of the Crab brings together intergenerational and intercultural conflict in a world of unknowns, deception, and loyalty. If anyone wants to catch a glimpse at the complexity of living in Puerto Rico after hurricanes and human-fabricated disasters, these stories are a must read. They take you through family friction and unconditional love, and the greatest betrayal with the gentleness of orégano brujo leaves."

—Yolanda Rivera Castillo

"The stories in this collection portray the many strains and pressures placed on family dynamics as they fragment and re-set in new circumstances. Partners struggle with differing conceptions of gender roles and conflicting ideals in our rapidly changing society. Parents facing conflicts in their own lives struggle to guide their children. The isolating effects of inner turmoil are explored, as well as the heightened sensitivity to the feeling of hurt that unleashes rage. The reader is mesmerized as seemingly ordinary and casual interactions escalate into psychological and physical violence."

—Carol M. Romey

Barbara Southard's stories locate themselves in the chaotic center of the colonial culture of Puerto Rico from the '70's to the present. They also resonate with fascinating, nuanced responses to feminism, family breakup, traditional machismo, police violence, corruption, and horrific natural disasters. Well after each story ends on the page, the reader remains caught in the powerful social and personal crosscurrents of the protagonist's struggles to navigate these rough waters of conflict with loved ones.

—Elena Lawton de Torruella

Excerpts from the book review of
THE PINCH OF THE CRAB
by Carmen Dolores Hernández,
El Nuevo Día, February 13, 2022

The Book of Betrayals

A married woman relives a terrible incident of her youth that her parents have chosen to ignore; a young woman discovers the true nature of the father who brought her up with love; a little boy faces violence—from animals, in the social environment, and that which lurks in the family—without really understanding what is happening; parents blame their son's friend for corrupting him when the truth is quite the opposite.

The ten stories in this book all revolve around betrayals. Especially painful betrayals that take place in the bosom of families that seem to be, if not happy, at least more or less normal. What provokes conflict is a change of perspective caused by failure to meet the usual expectations: parents who are not really protective; mothers who don't turn out to be so dedicated: the bitter discovery that love is not as enduring or as absolute as expected. The flaw—the crack in the polished surface of conventional expectations—has been there from the beginning, invisible to trusting eyes.

The story titled "Heavy Downpour" departs somewhat from this pattern. In this story, it is not the family or one of its members that betrays expectations of justice, but rather society itself that persecutes those who try to put justice into practice, threatening the established order by doing so. The character who appears in the house of a prosperous American housewife living in Puerto Rico, a friend from her rebellious youth, seems to present a threat to her and to the community, but that perception is erroneous. It is the political structure that betrays expectations of equity, justice and democracy. The issue is the political situation of Puerto Rico, apparently stable, although any challenge to this stability gives rise to institutional violence.

Southard writes in simple, straightforward English. Her style does not draw attention in and of itself; rather, it serves as a filter that allows us to "read" not only the significance of the words but the intentions that hide behind them that are not immediately apparent to the interlocutors within the stories. Moreover, she is good at handling premonitions, and also surprises, as in the story Fallen Branches, in which the action seems to point in one direction, but culminates in an unexpectedly explosive outcome.

(Translated from the original in Spanish with permission. See original in Appendices)

For my grandchildren

Shaila Malía Choudhury Madero
Yamir Andrés Choudhury Madero

Contents

The Pinch of the Crab 1
Tricky 17
Strike Three 35
Internal Injuries 61
Fallen Branches 81
Heavy Downpour 103
DNA Blues 111
Marcia and Mercedes 135
Neighbors 159
En el campo 181

APPENDICES

Acknowledgements 211
About the Author 213
Reseña (Book Review) 215

The Pinch of the Crab

Danny cried out and held on tight to his father's hand when the white foam of a real big one swept up the beach, tugging at his knees. After the wave receded, he pulled one foot and then the other out of the little mounds of sand left by the wash, and ran around his father to higher ground. He felt safer, but it was hard going in the soft sand.

As father and son passed the guest houses along Ocean Park in San Juan, Danny watched the big boys riding the waves. The surfers were left behind when they reached a calmer stretch of the ocean opposite Barbosa Park. His father stopped and put down two towels. Danny placed the bucket and shovel he was carrying next to the smaller one. Nearby, under the shade of a coconut tree, was a family gathering, complete with two huge coolers and a picnic basket.

"I'm thirsty," said Danny.

His father glanced up and down the beach, his brow furrowed, but there was no vendor in sight.

"We won't stay too long," he said.

"Mami always brings lemonade."

His father shrugged and took off his T-shirt. "Papito, ven conmigo. We'll cool off in the water."

The Pinch of the Crab

Danny eyed the waves. His father had told him they were calmer near the park, but they looked pretty big. He reached for his shovel. "Papi, I want to build a sandcastle."

"Okay, we'll swim later."

Danny started digging in the sand, while his father wiped the sweat off his brow with the palm of his hand, and stretched out on his towel, pulling the visor of his cap down. Danny worked hard, excavating a big hole to make a high wall. He glanced over at his father whose eyes were hidden.

"¡Mira, Papi! I'm building El Morro. Ayúdame."

Waking up with a start, his father pulled himself to a sitting position. Digging together, they made a fortress with a deep moat.

"We need a plastic cup to make the turrets," said his father.

Danny spied a crab scuttling along. He got up and chased the crab until it disappeared down a small hole, not even glancing at his father, who had found a discarded cup and was busy decorating the fort.

Danny grasped a twig and reached into the hole to tickle the crab. The little creature came out, mad, charging this way and that. Danny tried to catch him, but the crab was fast. He went back down his hole. Danny grabbed the plastic cup from his father's hand and plopped it down over another less wary crab. Scooping up his prisoner, he brought it over to the sandcastle and dumped it into the moat. The little crab tried valiantly to crawl out, but fell back each time.

"Pobrecito. He's trying to go back home."

Danny heard his father, but kept his eyes on the crab.

"I want to take him home with me," he cried, catching the crab in his right hand. He opened his fist slowly and watched, his eyes round, while the crab crawled slowly from palm to forearm.

"He likes me," said Danny, with a big smile, reaching out with his left hand to grab the crab. "Owwwwww." Feeling a hard pinch, Danny yanked his hand away. The crab fell to the ground and scuttled away.

Danny's face puckered up before he started to howl. His father crouched to get a better look at the red welt on his hand.

Between sobs Danny said, "It's going to bleed soon."

"Mijo, no es nada," said his father, smiling. "The skin's not broken. It'll be okay."

"I wanted to be his friend," said Danny, tears streaming down his cheeks, trying to hold back the sobs.

"But the crab didn't know that," his father pointed out. "He pinched because he was scared. He's a little guy. The two of us look very big to him."

Danny shook his head. His father's explanation hadn't made the bad feeling in his tummy go away. He put the hurt hand in his mouth. "I want to go home."

He stood there sucking his hand, while his father picked up the two towels and shook off the sand. Danny had to be told not to forget the pail and shovel. On the way back, he tried to fit his feet into his own backwards footprints.

Danny followed his father up the cement stairs of the beach access leading to an Ocean Park side street. At the top, he stopped and looked back, his eyes squinting against the blazing white sand and glints of sunlight dancing on the sea. His father was calling to him not to be such a slowpoke. Danny swallowed hard and stepped into the street where his father was waiting.

"How about a happy face?"

Danny tried hard to keep his mouth from quivering.

"Oye, hijito, crabs belong on the beach."

"I could put him in the fish tank."

His father smiled. "But the fish wouldn't like a crab in their tank."

Danny looked away. "The fish died," he said in a small voice.

"What? All of them?"

Danny nodded.

"Shit," said his father.

Danny dropped his father's hand. He wished he hadn't told the truth.

"Your mother didn't take care of them," said his father.

"Mami gave them food," said Danny. "They wouldn't eat."

Making an effort to control his annoyance, Carlos turned away from his son, and started walking, passing from bright sunlight into the shade of a line of flamboyán trees. While waiting for Danny to catch up, Carlos poked at the blossoms that carpeted the sidewalk with his foot. His former wife had asked him to leave the fish when he moved out, because Danny liked them so much.

Carlos reached for his son's hand and continued walking. He noticed a teenager who had been hidden from view by the thick trunk of a flamboyán tree. The youngster was standing just ahead on the grass between sidewalk and curb with his back toward them, facing an old Mitsubishi Mirage. Carlos and Danny stopped and watched the teenager fiddling with a screwdriver.

"Hey, got locked out?" Carlos asked.

The teenager whirled to face them, his face taut and hostile. Carlos tightened his hold on his son's hand. There had been an article in the paper yesterday about rising crime in the neighborhood, but this was just a boy and the car sure didn't look hot.

"Need some help?" said Carlos, keeping his voice easy.

The teenager's shoulders relaxed and he smiled, transforming the face of a possible juvenile delinquent into that of a friendly neighborhood kid.

"Gracias, señor. My brother left the key inside his car. I've almost got it open," he said, holding up the screwdriver, his tone confiding.

"Good luck," said Carlos.

The teenager turned back to apply himself to the job at hand, and Carlos tugged on his son's hand to resume walking. They had gone half a block when Carlos heard hurried footfalls. He turned and saw the teenager dodge between two parked cars and then cut in front of them on the sidewalk, running fast. Carlos looked back. A policeman was coming from behind them, pistol drawn.

"Papi," screamed Danny.

"Pa' abajo," yelled the cop, a tall thin fellow who gestured with his left hand for them to get on the ground while aiming at the fleeing teenager with the gun in his right.

The Pinch of the Crab

Carlos made a dive for the ground, pulling his son down with him, shielding the boy's head under his armpit.

"Shhhhh," he said to his son as the young cop vaulted over them and caught up with the teenager, bringing him down on the sidewalk.

A second cop, an older man with a large paunch, appeared out of nowhere. They pulled the teenager to a standing position. The thin cop felt him down while the burly one held the suspect's arms behind his back. The youngster started to struggle but then thought better of it and stood still.

"Anything on the sonofabitch?" asked the burly cop.

"Nah. He's clean," said the thin one, and then asked the teenager, "What's your name?"

"Tito."

"Cabrón. Your real name."

Carlos pulled himself up to a sitting position. The teenager still hadn't told the cops his name. He was just staring at them with a dazed expression on his face. The young cop hit the suspect hard with his open hand. As the sound of the slap died away, Carlos could hear the distant shouts of kids on the beach and then his son's agitated whisper. "Papi, they're hurting him."

The teenager was writhing in the burly cop's grip, unable to use his arms to protect his face.

"All right. Now tell us your name," said the young cop.

"Roberto Gómez, sir. It's my brother's car."

"Yeah," said the fat cop. "And your brother's the Mayor of San Juan."

"It's true," said the teenager. "I mean about the car. Ask him."

Both cops turned their heads to follow the finger pointing toward Carlos. Roberto took advantage of the split second when the cops' heads were turned to squirm out of the hold of the burly cop, and head butt the young one in the stomach, before taking off down the street. The young cop recaptured him within a hundred feet, the older cop close behind.

Carlos got to his feet. He could feel Danny clinging to his thigh. The cops beat Roberto until blood flowed down his face. Carlos glanced down and saw his son's eyes round with terror.

The force of the blows toppled Roberto onto the ground. The cops began to kick him viciously. Carlos grabbed his son in his arms and held him to his chest. Danny's high-pitched screams mingled in his ears with Roberto's low moans. The older cop stood still, wiping the sweat off his forehead, while the younger one landed a couple more.

"That's enough, Paco," he said, laying his hand on his colleague's arm.

The beating stopped. Roberto was silent, cowering on the ground, protecting his face with his hands, but Carlos could still hear Danny's cries.

The older cop turned toward Carlos and yelled, "Mira, take the kid out of here."

"Shhh," said Carlos to his son, putting his finger to his lips.

Danny kept still, except for low choking noises deep in his throat.

Carlos shifted the little boy's weight on to his hip, guiding Danny's long legs around his waist, and crossed the street as fast as he could. Once on the other side he turned, and saw the two policemen handcuffing Roberto. He quickly put his son's head down against his shoulder so Danny couldn't see while the policeman dragged the teenager toward a van.

At the corner, father and son turned onto a street parallel to the beach, losing sight of Roberto and the cops. Although Danny was heavy for a five-year-old, Carlos walked the three blocks to his apartment at a fast pace. Still carrying his son, he entered a gravel driveway. He had to bypass the main house in front with its well-manicured lawn and croton hedge to reach the annex. Carlos was breathing hard by the time he reached the landing in front of his second story apartment.

When his father tried to put him down on the landing, Danny wound his legs and arms tighter, and started crying again.

"Mira, you're not a baby anymore. You're a big boy."

Danny gulped hard, relaxed his grip and slid to the floor. He stood still while Carlos struggled to undo the knot to release the door key tied to the end of his towel.

"Damn key," said his father, turning it several times before the door finally opened.

When they stepped inside out of the bright sunlight, Danny could barely make out the outline of the sofa that his father was leading him to. It was scary. Once his father turned on the overhead light, Danny should have felt better, but he didn't. He wanted to sit on the big russet couch at home, the one you sink into, not this hard blue futon with the big coffee stain.

His father went into the kitchen to get him a glass of orange juice. Danny's tummy felt funny. He was no longer thirsty. His father sat down heavily beside him, and drank down a beer in a few gulps.

Danny looked down at the hand the crab had bitten, and gently rubbed the red spot.

"They hurt him real bad," he said.

His father put a coaster under Danny's orange juice glass, and then said with a smile, "Don't worry. They'll take him to the hospital. Drink your juice."

Danny took the glass handed to him, and put it down in front of him to one side of the coaster. He didn't want juice and he was not a baby. No.

"Roberto's not going to the hospital," he said in a loud voice. "He's going to *jail*."

His father put an arm around him.

"Tienes razón, mijo. After they take him to the doctor, he might have to go to jail. It's a crime to steal and even worse to attack a policeman."

"But he was scared."

"Who was scared?"

"Roberto."

His father was looking at him as though he didn't understand.

"They were bigger," said Danny. "Two big policemen."

"Danny, escúchame, the police don't put youngsters in jail, they put them in the Reformatory. It's like a school but much harder and you can't go home."

Danny could feel a lump in the back of his throat that hurt when he swallowed. He blinked to keep the tears from coming. "He won't eat in Formatory," he told his father. "He'll die."

"He'll be fine. I promise you."

Carlos took Danny in his lap, and gently stroked his hair. Danny stopped crying. His head was buried in his father's shoulder when the doorbell rang.

"Must be your mother," said Carlos, leaning over to get a Kleenex for Danny to blow his nose before answering the door. Danny watched from the sofa while his parents exchanged pecks on the cheek, and then ran to his mother when she opened her arms wide. She had on a blue blouse, and smelled of flowers as always.

Before he knew it, his mother was holding him at arm's length, watching him intently. "¿Qué pasó? You've been crying."

Danny looked at his father uncertainly.

His mother was looking at his father, too, with a bright smile on her face. "Cuéntame Carlos, what did you guys do today?"

"Nothing much," said his father. "Tú sabes, lo de siempre. We went to the beach for a while."

"Did you swim?" asked his mother, looking at Danny.

Danny ignored the question. "A big crab bit me," he said.

His mother shifted her eyes from Danny to his father. "Is he hurt?"

"No," said Carlos. "Believe me, it was an itsy-bitsy crab."

"Show me where it bit you, Danny."

After a careful examination, his mother gave his hand a big kiss to make it all better. Danny wasn't so sure. He put two fingers of the hurt hand in his mouth, expecting his mother to remind him that big boys don't do that, but she wasn't paying attention to him anymore.

"Carlos, we have to talk," she said.

His father shifted his weight from one foot to the other. "Okay. I'm listening."

"Mami, Mami," cried Danny.

The Pinch of the Crab

"Shhh! Shhh! Just one moment, Danny. This is big people talk." His mother turned away and told his father in a loud voice, "Óyeme. Yesterday, I got a notice from the Montessori School that the fees will go up. You've got to help out more."

His father answered very softly. "Maritere, you know my office has been really slow. We'll see."

Danny interrupted. "Mami, Mami, you know what we saw…"

"Dios mío, Danny, callate."

Danny looked to his father for help, but Carlos winked at him, a very small wink, and said, "Mijo, don't interrupt your mother."

His mother's eyes were again focused on his father. "We'll see. We'll see. That's what you always say. That's not good enough."

Danny cut in before Carlos could reply. "It still hurts, Mami."

Maritere sighed. "I'll put a band-aid on it when we get home. Kiss Papi good-bye."

Danny gave his father a big hug and kiss, and then walked out the door hand in hand with his mother. She stopped on the landing, turned around and said: "Carlos, promise me you'll think about it. Education is very important. And don't forget to bring the check tomorrow."

The next morning it was hard for Danny to wake up for school. His mother had to yell at him to get dressed quick, not make her late for work. He dawdled over breakfast, not eating, just pouring syrup to make spirals on his oatmeal. His mother asked whether he was feeling okay. Danny said he was fine, but his tummy wasn't hungry.

After looking at her watch, Maritere gave up getting him to eat. They were about to get into the car when she noticed Danny had forgotten his lunch box. They had to run back into the building and go up the elevator to the apartment.

The Pinch of the Crab

When they got back to the car, his mother buckled him into the booster seat in the back. Danny wanted to tell her that he was too big for a booster seat, but the way she threw the lunch box into the car, and told him he would get her fired, made him hold his tongue. They drove to school in silence.

Maritere pulled over near a house with a neatly manicured lawn and an iron gate painted dark blue. A tree with bright green leaves was painted below red and blue letters. His mother had told him the sign said Wisdom Tree Montessori School.

While Maritere maneuvered to get closer to the curb, Danny kept his eye on the front driveway. The two boys who had told him booster seats are for babies were nowhere to be seen.

When his mother turned around to unsnap his seatbelt, Danny gave her a kiss, shouldered his book bag and ran to the gate. The principal, an older woman with white hair, was just opening it for him when Danny remembered. He raced back to the car calling, "¡Mami! ¡Mami! The habichuelas for the children in the flood!"

Maritere hit her head with her hand. "Ay bendito, I left them in a bag on the kitchen table. I told you to remind me, Danny."

"We have to go back, Mami."

"I can't. I'm already late for work."

"Please, Mami, please. The children don't have food."

"Danny, escúchame, I've got an important meeting. You don't want me to lose my job."

"Mami, Mami, they'll die."

"Tell the teacher we'll bring the cans tomorrow."

"No, that's too late."

The principal came up and took Danny's hand. His mother turned the steering wheel, waved to Danny and rode off. Danny stood for a moment staring at where the car had been, close to tears, but then he caught sight of José and Charlie and entered the open gate with his two friends. They walked through the carport to the backyard.

The Pinch of the Crab

Danny was happy to see Missie Rodríguez, his favorite teacher, on yard duty with the kids that arrived before eight. He followed her instructions to put his book bag and lunch box under the large banyan tree. José and Charlie put their book bags down next to Danny's.

Charlie announced that he had bubble gum, but whoever wants some will have to catch me first. They raced around the yard until Charlie finally gave them each a packet. Pedro came running over to ask for one, too. They all started playing catch, but Danny's tummy still wasn't feeling good. He sat down on an elevated root of the banyan tree next to his book bag. The bubble gum didn't taste good anymore, so he took it out of his mouth and stuck it to the root.

That was when Danny noticed the spaghetti can peeking out of the top of José's book bag. He glanced around. Missie Rodríguez was in the carport, talking to a little girl, her back toward Danny. Cautiously, he moved his hand closer. José and Charlie were busy with their game and Pedro, who was nowhere to be seen, must have gone into the school already. Danny grabbed the spaghetti can and put it in his own book bag.

"I saw you. I saw you."

It was Pedro, hiding behind the banyan tree. Danny sat quietly, pretending Pedro must be talking to someone else.

"Hey, José, Danny stole your can."

"Did not."

José and Charlie came running over. José checked his bag. The two Goya chick pea cans were still there, but the spaghetti can was missing. Danny grabbed his own bag, but it wasn't latched and the spaghetti can rolled out. José made a dive for it and held on tight.

"Give it back," screamed Danny. "It's mine. My mother bought it yesterday at Pueblo."

José, who was holding the can up high over his head, looked uncertain, and let his arm drop.

Pedro yelled. "I saw him. He stole it."

The Pinch of the Crab

Danny made a lunge for the can and got it back. José punched him. Danny let go of the can to punch back. Charlie pushed him to the ground. Suddenly, the three of them were rolling on the ground and dirt was entering Danny's open mouth, granular on his tongue and bitter tasting. Then Danny was on the bottom getting pummeled by Charlie while José held him down.

Danny pushed with all his might against the arms that were pinning him to the ground. No deal. José was bigger.

Pedro's singsong was rattling in his ears. "Danny is a thief. I'm going to tell."

Danny jerked his head up off the ground, jutting out his lower jaw to reach the arm jamming his chest, not letting him breathe, and bit down hard.

José let out a bloodcurdling yell and let go.

Danny sat up and gasped for air. Missie Rodríguez was there looking at the bite mark. The blood was dripping down José's arm. Frightened, Danny began to cry, but no one noticed.

Missie Rodríguez was cradling José in her arms, while another teacher applied bandages, and Charlie and Pedro told them about the stolen can. The two teachers carried the bleeding boy into the school. After a couple of minutes, they came back for Danny. He grabbed onto the big banyan root, but it was hard to get a good grip. They dragged him into the principal's office, screaming that it wasn't his fault.

In the early evening of the same day, Danny was seated on the russet couch in the living room watching cartoons. His mother, who had taken their supper plates into the kitchen, was talking on the phone. Danny couldn't hear the words, but he knew she was crying. He pulled a soft side pillow close to his chest. His eye hurt. Gingerly, he touched the lid of his right eye and then his left. They felt different.

The Pinch of the Crab

His mother came in and switched the TV off. Her eyes were red.

"Danny, we have to talk."

"Mami, my eye hurts."

She turned on the corner table light. "Let's have a look. Which one hurts?"

Danny pointed to his left eye, the one that felt puffy.

"It's a little swollen. Let me get you the ice pack."

Maritere went into the kitchen. When she came back and applied the pack, Danny cried out. It was too cold.

"Here, hold it yourself. You're a big boy."

Danny didn't want to, but he kept the ice pack on for a long time. Finally, his mother said. "That's enough. It'll be better in the morning."

"No, it won't," said Danny, pressing the pack to his eye again. "I can't go to school."

His mother shook her head, and took the ice pack from him. "You can't go to school anyway. You're suspended for a week. Danny, we have to talk about what you did. Why did you take José's can? Answer me. And don't lie."

"I didn't steal it. I just wanted one for the flood children."

"No te entiendo, Danny. You never bit anyone before. Tell me why."

"He..."

"Escúchame, Danny, José's parents had to take him to Emergency. He needed stitches."

Danny's eyes wandered away from his mother's face to stare at the Lion King poster. Finally, he said in a small voice, "Mami, can you stay home with me tomorrow?"

Maritere sighed. "No. My boss will kill me. You can stay with your father. He's off on Tuesdays."

Danny sat up in the bed with a wild look in his eyes and yelled, "NO! NO! Not Papi's!"

"Danny, what's wrong? What happened? Did your father hit you?"

Danny shook his head. His father wasn't like that.

The Pinch of the Crab

"Por el amor de Dios, tell me what's wrong with you."

"They'll put me in Formatory," Danny said.

"What are you talking about?"

"The two policemen."

"What policemen?"

"Near Papi's. They have guns and they put kids in Formatory."

Danny began to cry softly. Maritere stroked his hair soothingly. "Mijo, créeme, the police don't care about fights in school. Don't worry."

Danny must have fallen asleep on the couch, because the last thing he remembered was his mother stroking his hair. He woke up in his own bed. For a moment, he thought it must be time to get dressed for school, but then he realized it was nighttime. He lay very still listening to the drumming of rain on the metal louvers of his bedroom window. The bad feeling in his tummy was back.

The doorbell rang. Danny sat up, his body tense. Maybe his mother was wrong about the police not caring about fights in school. Then he heard his father's voice.

"Here's the check."

"Why don't you ever pick up when I call?" His mother was speaking in a whisper that didn't hide her angry voice.

"I saw your number on my cell and came right over with the check," said Carlos.

"Come in. I have to talk to you." Now his mother's voice was friendly. Danny got up from bed and walked toward the door, which was slightly ajar.

"I can't come in now, Maritere," said his father. "There's someone waiting for me in the car."

"I don't care who's waiting for you," said his mother. Her voice cracked. Not knowing whether she was mad or sad, Danny stayed put. "You can't just hand over a check and walk off when there's a problem," she yelled at his father. "I need to talk to you about your son."

"Is Danny okay?" asked Carlos.

"NO, HE'S NOT OKAY. He bit someone in school. They had to take the kid to Emergency. Danny's suspended."

"Maritere, don't worry. At his age boys are always getting into fights. He's a good kid. It'll be okay."

Danny came running out. His father, still standing in the doorway, swept him up and cradled him on his shoulder.

"Papi, I didn't bite José on purpose. He..."

Danny wanted to explain that he didn't mean to hurt his friend, but he couldn't find the words to describe the way José held him down until it was hard to breathe, or how scary it was to be attacked by two kids at once.

His mother wiped tears off her face with her hand and said to his father, "Danny keeps talking about policemen. Did something happen that you didn't tell me about?"

Danny took a deep breath. His father put him down on the floor.

"Carlos, for God's sake tell me."

Carlos just stood there for a long moment, tugging at his shirt collar. "We were coming back from the beach, tú sabes, on that street with beach access. Two policemen arrested a car thief. The guy was pretty young. A teenager. They roughed him up. Danny was upset."

"Why in hell didn't you tell me before?"

"I was going to, but you wouldn't let me. You insisted on talking about more child support."

"That's so like you. You mess up, don't tell me what's happened, and then blame me. Nunca es tu culpa. Now you don't have to worry about the Montessori School's fees going up, because they'll probably kick Danny out for good."

Maritere was crying, and waving her arms. "All because of you," she screamed.

The Pinch of the Crab

His father stepped back into the hallway of the building. His mother slammed the door, and sat down on the couch, cradling her head in her hands. Danny couldn't see her face.

The drumming of raindrops on the metal louvers had stopped. There was a light tap on the door.

"Don't open it," said his mother.

Danny stood still, staring at the closed door. "Papi, the crab didn't mean to hurt me," he said.

A chorus of coquis muffled the footfalls retreating down the hallway.

"It was two against one," Danny whispered.

Tricky

Someone was shaking her bed. Stop it! What's wrong? Stop it! STOP IT! Then the rumbling began. Irene opened her eyes. Pitch dark.

"¡Mami! ¡Papi! Help me!"

She lifted herself out of bed. Her toe caught in the sheet and she fell backwards. The floor was cold, and it heaved back and forth. She pulled herself up and ran toward the door, her body pitching this way and that. Where's the doorknob?

"¡Mami! ¡Papi! Let me out! Let me out!!!"

Irene beat her hands on the door. Suddenly she was in her father's arms.

"Cálmate hija. It's over. The earthquake is over. You're okay."

Irene could hear her own sharp intake of breath. She was panting as though she had run a mile on the beach. Her mom switched on the overhead light. The three of them stood together, arms wound around each other. Their bodies felt warm. Irene cried quietly. It was over. She was safe.

Irene fell asleep on her parents' bed. When she awoke, her mom said there had been an aftershock at daybreak, but Irene had slept through it. She got up and joined her parents in the living room of their apartment where they were having coffee. Her mom brought Irene hot chocolate and a chocolate-covered doughnut and sat down next to her on the sofa. A newscaster on the TV, a heavyset man with a moustache, was pointing

The Pinch of the Crab

to a map of Puerto Rico with concentric circles marking the epicenter of the quake.

Her mom shuddered and pulled Irene close. "The damage in the south is horrible. But thank the Lord, nothing major here in San Juan."

"But, Mami, it felt like our whole building was going to collapse," said Irene.

"The taller the building the more it sways," said her dad. "The sway is scary, but that flexibility is what keeps the building from falling."

On the TV, the newscaster with the pointer was replaced by scenes of destruction in the south.

"Oh no," said her mom, staring at the screen. "Look what happened in Ponce."

Her dad looked at her mom, his eyebrows scrunched in a straight line. "For God's sake, Isabel, change the channel."

"Papi, I'm not a baby. I'm twelve years old," said Irene, leaning forward to see. A small two-story house, built on pillars over the garage, had collapsed, crushing the two cars beneath. The TV camera lingered over the concrete rubble, car fenders and parts of wooden kitchen cabinets scattered over the front yard.

"Did they all die?" Irene wanted to know. There were no bodies in the debris. Maybe the people were okay.

"I'm sure the family had already left," said her mom. "You know there were lots of small quakes in the south before this big one, so they probably came to San Juan to stay with relatives."

Well, maybe. Images of the collapsed house had given way to an apartment building with a balcony hanging perilously over the street below. Her dad switched off the TV.

Leaving her doughnut half eaten, Irene got up and went to the balcony. The view from their Condado apartment was partially blocked by another condominium, but she could see the ocean. The waves looked normal, not unusually big, and a pelican was diving for fish. He finally got one and gulped it down before rising back into the sky. Looked like the earthquake was no big deal for the pelican. But could it be a mother pelican? Maybe she had a nest in a mangrove, and the earthquake had shaken the tree so badly that the nest fell down. Would the baby birds die?

The next day Irene awoke to the sound of her mother's voice screaming. "I don't want to hear it, Adrián. You've made up your mind, and nothing will change it. Stop blaming me. It takes two to tango, and two to un-tango, doesn't it? But you want to get a few more shots in, don't you?"

Her parents were fighting again. The truce was over. It had lasted all of twenty-four hours after the quake. It was already nine o'clock. Irene had overslept, but no one had called her. She brushed her teeth, got dressed slowly and padded down the hallway.

"Mami, why…?" Irene had been about to ask why she wasn't awakened for school, but she stopped mid-sentence. A large blue suitcase, a small brown one and her father's briefcase were standing next to the front door.

"Papi, you can't go," Irene screamed. "What if there's another one? Papi, please."

Adrián came, gathered her up in his arms, and sat her down next to him on the sofa. When her sobs quieted, he explained patiently that the decision to separate from her mother had already been taken. He reminded her that it didn't mean her parents didn't care for each other—it was just that they couldn't get along, couldn't live in the same house.

"And we both love you more than anything in the world. This way you won't have to witness endless arguments. You will be happier. All of us will be happier."

"But you can't go now. A bigger one will come. The whole building will collapse. Like in the movie. You know, the one you and Mami watched. Don't go! Don't go! Stay with me!"

"What movie? Irene, what are you talking about?"

"The one on Netflix about the earthquake in Mexico. 7:19, or something like that. You remember. The man was buried under the building. He had blood on his face. One eye was red and his legs were caught under a concrete slab, and it was all dark but he had a flashlight…"

"Irene, that was different. No comparison. That was a much bigger earthquake."

Irene listened to all his counter arguments, quietly explained in her father's sensible voice. The epicenter of the earthquake activity in Puerto Rico was in the south, far from San Juan. There might be a few aftershocks, but the main event was over. Besides, real life is not like what you see on TV. Not to be afraid.

But he was wrong! No use arguing though. She would have to sit through a long discussion of epicenters and seismological data, nodding her head as her father made each point, and in the end he would leave anyway. She went to her room and lay back down on the unmade bed. If he didn't come to kiss her goodbye, she would hate him forever.

He did come, called her by her pet name, Rennie, embraced and kissed her. She could hear his footfalls going down the hall, and the front door latch. She rolled over and closed her eyes. Then she jumped up, and ran to open the front door, screaming, "The big one is coming, Papi, the big one is coming, don't leave!"

No one was in front of the elevator. It was descending, 10, 9, 8, 7, 6…

Back in the apartment, all was quiet, except the hum of distant waves breaking. The door to her parents' room was closed. Irene moved close to the door and heard her mother's sobs. She returned to the living room and sat on the same sofa on which her father had explained everything to her.

Isabel came out, and sat next to her. "It's just the two of us, now."

Irene pulled away. "Why didn't you tell Papi to stay? At least another week, until we're sure the quakes are over."

"It wouldn't do any good, Irene, you know that."

Irene nodded and let her mother draw her into her arms.

The going was rough for the next few days. Irene's school was closed because engineers had to check that it was safe after the earthquake. Isabel's office was closed, too. Mother and daughter didn't do much of anything, but sit around in the living room looking at their phones, or watching TV.

There were only two apartments to a floor. Theirs was 11B and the neighbor's apartment was 11A. From the living room, Irene could hear the elevator door open and close, and then the muffled sound of footfalls, but no one rang their doorbell.

He's not coming back.

Irene got up and walked to the balcony. Not a pelican in sight.

But then things got better. One morning, she found her mom in the kitchen. "Why are you making sandwiches? It's not lunchtime."

"Nope. Hey, we're going for a picnic at Luquillo beach. Quick, get yourself some cereal to eat, while I finish packing our lunch. Let's get an early start before it gets too crowded."

Even though it was January, the water was warm, and the waves were not too big for swimming. After eating their sandwiches, they bought ice creams from a vendor and then lay sunning together. Irene sighted a huge pelican in the sky and pointed him out to her mom.

"That's not a pelican. Look at the forked tail. Tijerilla, scissor bird. Magnificent frigate bird in English."

Irene was impressed. How come her mom knew so much about birds? Isabel explained that her best friend at Princeton loved birds and the two of them went on bird-watching expeditions at Cape May in New Jersey with field glasses. "I still have them, two pairs. Don't let me forget to bring them next time."

They started going to the beach every other day, or bike riding on the paths in Piñones, always with field glasses around their necks. It was so much fun that Irene felt sad when school reopened. Well, not really, once she sighted her best friend, Paola.

On his weekends, her dad picked her up on Saturday at two o'clock. The first time she went with her dad, her mom hardly talked while they were eating lunch.

"Mami, are you okay? You look sad."

"I'll miss you, but don't worry, go have a great time with your dad. He should be here in 15 minutes. Are you packed?"

The time with her dad was fun, too. He took her to the movies on Saturday, and they went to eat at a restaurant in the mountains with the best mofongo on the island on Sunday. Her dad was cheerful all the time, asking her about school, laughing with the waitress. Maybe, he was right. Divorce isn't all that bad.

After the mofongo, Irene ordered coconut flan for dessert and her father ordered coffee. He took a sip, and said you can't beat the flavor of good Puerto Rican coffee. Irene asked for a sip. She made a face and handed it back. Her dad smiled at her.

"How is your mother doing?"

"She's okay."

"What do you do when you're alone with her?"

Why should it matter to him? He left, took his suitcases and walked out. "We go biking a lot. Why do you want to know?"

"Irene, you sound mad at me. Look, just because we are getting a divorce doesn't mean I don't care about your mother. I do care. I'm asking how she's doing because she has suffered severe depression. Do you know what depression means?"

Well, yeah. She did know, because her dad was a psychologist and he had told her all about patients with depression. Not just ordinary sadness, because something bad happens, but sadness that doesn't go away.

"Irene, I asked you a question."

"Yeah, I know what depression is. It's bad, but not as awful as schizo, you know schizofrenk."

"Schizophrenia."

"Whatever. I don't remember Mami ever being depressed. Sad, yes."

"You're right. There's a difference." Her dad smiled at her. "But your mom did go through a depression. You wouldn't remember because you were too young." He took another sip of coffee, placed it back on the saucer, and said in a low voice. "She suffered from postpartum depression."

Irene said nothing.

Her father shook his head. "Sorry, I don't know why I told you that. Forget about it. It was a long time ago."

Irene said OK, let's talk about something else, but she knew as soon as she was alone, her finger would touch the Google app on her phone. She didn't get the spelling right the first time, but postpartum depression appeared among the choices. Irene wished she hadn't looked. She knew her mother loved her. How could she have fallen into a depression when Irene was born? Something about hormones. The science teacher had talked about hormones and glands but she couldn't remember much. It was a relief when Paola called to ask whether she understood the social studies assignment.

She put the whole shitty depression subject out of her mind until she overheard her mom talking with her best friend, Gladys, on the phone. "Oye, chica, listen to me, I swear I'm fine. Me siento como una persona nueva. You have to believe me. I had the blues for a couple of days, but I'm not depressed. You know what I've been doing? Getting out of the apartment. Going to the beach, biking with Irene, bird-watching. We love it." Isabel smiled at her daughter, got up from the sofa, and started walking down the hallway. Before the bedroom door closed, Irene caught the last words. "Nothing like nature to make you forget misery over a man."

Well, that explained why they were always going on nature expeditions. Whatever. Her mom enjoyed the expeditions. She enjoyed them. The science teacher was impressed because Irene knew so much about birds and manatees. It was all good.

Isn't there a saying that good things don't last forever? Two months later, in March, everything changed. Her mom used to take her cell phone to the bedroom to talk with Gladys about the divorce, but then she began beating those hasty retreats whenever the word Coronavirus came up.

Irene got exasperated. "Mami, you don't have to leave the room. It's all over TV. My science teacher talked to us about Coronavirus in class, yesterday. I'm old enough to understand. He said school will probably be closed next week."

Later that same day Isabel got a message saying that Irene's school would be closed indefinitely. But not to worry. Irene would be able to finish sixth grade. There would be classes online. Isabel's boss called and said she would be working from home as long as the law firm still had enough business and could pay its junior lawyers.

Irene's grandmother came to visit a few days later, and the three of them sat in the living room watching Governor Mayra Sánchez speaking on TV, explaining the decision to impose a curfew and a lockdown of everything except essential services, like supermarkets. The governor spoke earnestly, her tone reassuring. Irene was impressed. She liked her long hair, blondish white, and the different colored masks she wore that always matched her clothes. The governor would take care of everyone, not let anyone get Coronavirus.

Grandma praised the governor for taking action early, shutting down everything before the virus spread. Mayra Sánchez was doing her best in a difficult situation. To Irene's surprise, her mother took a very different view.

"How can you say she's doing her best? Yeah, sure. We the citizens all have to stay home, keep social distancing. We have to sacrifice. But we do our part, keep social distancing, maybe lose our jobs, and what is the government doing? Have they worked out a tracing system? NO. Have they done enough testing? NO. NO, NO."

"Cálmate, hija. These things take time. Governor Sánchez is trying."

"How can I stay calm? Our government sees the virus as a new opportunity for corruption. Give political contributors big contracts to supply tests at exorbitant prices. Ordinary people sacrifice while they make money."

Isabel got up and left the room. Irene went over to the sofa and hugged her grandmother. Then she remembered about social distancing and went back to her own seat on the easy chair. When her mom came back her eyes were red. Grandma hugged her close. Her mom said she was sorry, she didn't mean to yell, it was just all so depressing.

Irene was upset. Could it be true that the governor was messing things up? On TV, she looked so good, so caring, like an older auntie. What if she was just pretending to be concerned, but really doing nothing to protect us? After her grandmother left, Irene went to her room and called her dad. He told her not to worry about testing and tracing. It takes a while to set these things up. Even in the States they don't have effective tracing yet. Only in South Korea. The thing is to follow the governor's rules of social distancing to the letter. That's the way to be safe. Irene promised she would.

"Did you say something about your grandmother?" he asked.

"Yeah. Mami was arguing with her."

"On the phone?"

"No. Grandma came by to give us more masks."

Her dad exploded. He didn't pick up Irene last weekend because he had seen patients too recently for it to be safe. What in hell was her mom doing letting her mother come over? Irene said Grandma always wore a mask, but her father paid no attention. He was fine with her mom having custody as long as she acted like a responsible parent. But he wasn't going to let anyone put his daughter in danger. Then he apologized. "Sweetie, it's just that I want you to be safe. Don't worry. I'll talk to your mom."

After her dad hung up, Irene sat on her bed, hugging her knees and rocking back and forth. What had she done? Why couldn't she learn to keep her mouth shut? Now, her parents would have another big fight. Even worse, her grandmother wouldn't be able to move in with them. She wanted Grandma to come. Her mom had no time to help with her online schooling, because she always had to work. And her mom was sad all the time again. So much for divorce being better, everyone living happily ever after.

Her dad kept his word about calling her mom. She couldn't hear his voice, but by the way her mom screamed it must have been him. "Listen, don't tell me how to protect my daughter. I'm being extremely careful. I made my mother give me an exact accounting of the last time she saw anyone, you know, her last social contact. What do you think I am? An idiot?

The Pinch of the Crab

You're the irresponsible parent, not me. You left right after the earthquake, when your daughter was panicked, freaked out, didn't you? So anxious to leave, you couldn't wait a few days until she calmed down. Don't threaten me with lawyers and custody suits. You're a hypocrite! You're not worried about your daughter, you just want to get me, make me suffer. Shut up! I don't have to talk to you anymore."

After this conversation, her mother became even sadder and more withdrawn. Isabel spent all her time in her bedroom at her computer. She hardly talked to Irene, except to tell her to wash her hands. Not so fast she would say, you have to work up a lather first, then wash your whole hand, get in between the fingers, and soap up to your elbows. Irene learned to linger for a long time in the bathroom when washing her hands.

When she came out to sit in the living room, her mom wasn't interested in anything except watching the news on TV to find out how many new cases of Coronavirus there were on the island, and how many respirators were available in the hospitals. Irene busied herself with games on her cellphone while Isabel muttered that the numbers cited by the government weren't accurate. There were probably twice or three times as many cases.

Irene thought about those happier days when they used to go bird-watching. She looked for the field glasses in the hall closet and went out on the balcony. "Mami, look," she cried, "the frigate bird!" Her mom nodded, looked briefly and went back to her phone. Irene searched the bookshelf for the guidebook about Caribbean birds.

"Do you remember that bird we saw with the curved beak and the very long tail? Look, this is it—the Puerto Rican cuckoo!" She handed her mom the book.

"Be careful, Rennie. We shouldn't be handling the same book. Leave it open on the table and I'll look at it tomorrow."

The book stayed open on the table. No one looked at it the next day. A whole week went by. The cuckoo, proudly holding a lizard in his claw, was still there, waiting for someone to look at him when Grandma appeared with a large suitcase. Irene started toward her, but then she remembered.

Social distancing. Her mom would scream at her if they got too close. But it was still great to have Grandma here. Maybe her mom would start acting like her mom again. But did her dad know?

Adrián came to pick her up the next Saturday. While father and daughter were eating supper together, take-out from her favorite Italian restaurant, he asked how her mother and grandmother were doing. Irene tried to read his face. Did that mean he had no objection to Grandma moving in with them?

"They're fine," said Irene. "Well, Mami's kinda sad. I try to cheer her up."

"Really? Even after your grandmother came to stay?"

"I think Mami's getting better."

That was a lie. Well, maybe, you could say that her mom felt better for the first few days after Grandma came, but after that it had been all downhill.

Her mom rarely came out of her room. Office work was her excuse. But sometimes when Irene called her to come and eat, she found her mother sitting doing nothing, her eyes fixed on the window that faced the ocean. She didn't even watch TV anymore. The news was too depressing, she said. She stayed in her nightgown all day, and her hair looked like it had never been brushed. Was this the same person who had taught Irene the importance of good taste? You put on a touch of makeup to bring out your best features, but not too much. You dress stylishly, but don't just get what everyone's buying, get what looks good on you.

Isabel's boss called and said she could take two weeks of paid sick leave, but he wouldn't be able to pay her salary after that unless they got new business. Now that she didn't have to work on her computer, Irene thought her mom would come out of her room, join her and her grandma playing dominos, or help her with math. Grandma was no good at explaining how to convert decimals into fractions. There were online videos, but Irene had a hard time concentrating on them. She was doing fine in everything else, but math was dragging her down. What would her dad say? He had always taught her not to make excuses. If you work hard, you will get good grades. It's that simple.

Her mom never went out of the house except for the weekly shopping. Irene wanted to go with her but she said no. Isabel came back with six bags. Irene went into the kitchen to help. Don't touch them! Stay away! Irene stood in the doorway while her mother scrubbed each item with sanitizer individually. Fresh fruits were washed repeatedly with dish soap and then again with sanitizer before being put in the refrigerator.

"The supermarket was awful," her mother said. "People don't wear their masks correctly, and they get too close. What's the matter with everyone? You're supposed to stay six feet away. I was picking out oranges, and this man comes up right next to me. I told him to get back until I finished. What an idiot! Putting himself and everyone else in danger!"

The following week was worse. Irene could hear her mother crying quietly while sanitizing all the food items in the kitchen. Her grandmother called out, "Isa, please let me help," but her mom yelled for her to say away. Sobbing uncontrollably, she finally emerged from the kitchen. "Don't anyone get near me!"

"Okay, okay," said Grandma. "Isa, please sit down in the dining room for a moment and tell us what's wrong. We'll stay here in the living room."

Isabel reached for a chair and held onto it as though to steady herself. "There was this idiot in the cheese section. A young guy, tall and skinny with long hair. He had a mask, but it didn't cover his nose properly, you could see blackheads. Then he sneezed, and the mask came off. I could see droplets rising in the air coming toward me."

Then the story got very confusing. The droplets were large and pink but they changed color in the light, rainbow colors, and they didn't stop coming after Isabel. She left the shopping cart in the middle of the aisle and ran to the other end of the store. The droplets rose into the air like clouds and dispersed in whirls all over the store.

"I know you don't believe me, but there were clouds of droplets everywhere, slowly dripping down, contaminating everyone. And when I went

Tricky

to the other side of the store, the clouds kept chasing me. I had to get you both something to eat so I ran out and went to another store. Don't come near me, I'm contaminated. I've got Covid-19."

Isabel ran into her bedroom and locked the door. Irene and her grandmother tried to persuade her to come out, or at least to eat something. No luck! Finally, Grandma put a thermometer in front of the closed bedroom door. Take your temperature every four hours and let us know, she said.

That night Isabel wouldn't eat anything. The next day Grandma made breakfast, but she wouldn't come out. Irene tried to take the breakfast tray into her room, but her mother screamed at her. "Stay out, stay out. I'm contaminated." They became accustomed to leaving her mother's meals in a tray in front of her door.

A whole week went by this way.

"Do you think Mami really saw droplets all over the store?" Irene asked her grandmother.

"Well, I'm not sure. Your mom had a bad shock in the supermarket when that careless man sneezed all over the place. People should be careful—look out for one another. But nowadays it's everyone for himself."

"But wouldn't other people in the store have seen the droplet clouds if they were really there? Mami could have been imagining things."

"Well, people imagine things all the time." Her grandmother smiled. "I seem to remember that you had an imaginary friend when you were five years old."

"Grandma, that was a long time ago."

"What was your friend's name? Paquito, wasn't it?"

"Yeah, but I didn't see visions of him."

"You sure talked about him a lot. But you grew out of it. Your mom will get over this too. Don't worry. She just needs time to get over the shock."

Her grandma thought everything would be okay, but Irene was worried. A year ago, she had joined her mom while she was watching the film *A Beautiful Mind* on Netflix. The man was a brilliant mathematician

The Pinch of the Crab

but he saw visions and heard voices. Her dad said the movie was about schizophrenia, and it wasn't appropriate for a kid her age. What was her mother thinking letting her watch it? But it really wasn't all that scary, and the man got better at the end, so people who see visions can get better.

Irene wondered whether she should tell her father about her mom's vision. If she did, he would start talking about lawyers and child custody. Better to keep quiet. But he's a psychologist. He'll know whether it's okay to see rainbow-colored sneeze droplets in a supermarket. On her next weekend with him, she asked him to explain what schizophrenia is.

"Why this sudden interest in schizophrenia?"

"Just curious. I understand what depression is, but you never told me much about schizophrenia."

Adrián explained that schizophrenia is a more serious condition that may involve hearing voices or seeing visions.

"You mean, it's like imagining things? I remember having an imaginary friend when I was little."

Her dad smiled. "Wasn't his name Paquito? But don't worry sweetheart. Lots of kids have imaginary friends, especially only children. They get lonely because they have no brothers and sisters. Usually, they grow out of it once they start school. But you always knew Paquito wasn't real. That's the difference. People with schizophrenia think their visions are real."

"But they get better, don't they?"

"Well, not always. Some schizophrenics have to take pills all their lives and others have to be institutionalized—you know, put in hospitals for care. But what brought this on? Why are your worrying about schizophrenia?"

"I just wanted to know." After a pause, Irene added. "It was something my friend Paola said."

"About who?"

Irene almost said Paola was worried about her mother, but she thought better of it, and said it was about an older cousin.

Tricky

"Did she say what her cousin's symptoms are?"

"It's all about Coronavirus. If someone sneezes or coughs, she sees clouds of droplets in rainbow colors going around infecting people, or something like that."

"Well, droplets do go around infecting people but they usually aren't visible. I'd say it's a borderline case. If her cousin keeps on seeing this type of vision, or has other illusions, she should see a psychiatrist."

This conversation was not reassuring. Irene got even more freaked out when she heard her mom talking in a low voice. She sidled up to the closed bedroom door, but she couldn't make out the words, her mom's voice was too low. Of course, she could be talking on the phone. But suppose she was hearing voices, and talking back to them?

It took a long time for Isabel to come out of hiding. The first hopeful sign was when she allowed Irene to enter her room to put the dinner tray on the small chest of drawers located far from the bed.

"Mami, how are you feeling?"

"Better. I've been following Grandma's instructions to take my temperature, and so far, no fever."

"That's good Mami, isn't it? Doesn't that mean you're not infected?'

"I hope so, but we have to wait a while to be sure, sweetheart. I miss you terribly. If only I could hug you, hold you close!"

Irene nodded, and fought back tears. Her mom missed her, needed her. At the door she turned back, touched her fingers to her lips and waved a kiss.

"I love you, too," her mom said, waving back a kiss. "But don't forget to wash your hands."

"I will."

Afterwards, Isabel began joining them for meals, even playing a game or two of dominos. "Sorry, I've been in hiding so long," she told Irene. "I was so worried that I had caught the virus and I would infect you and Grandma. I guess I overreacted to what happened in the store. I'll try to be a better mother to you, I promise."

Irene went over and gave her mom a big hug, then drew back, afraid her mom would scold her for not respecting social distancing, but Isabel clutched her close and began to cry softly.

Everything went back to normal. Her mom told Grandma to rest, she would do the cooking.

"Okay," said Grandma, "but leave the shopping to me. I don't want you going to the supermarket."

"No, I'll go. People over sixty should stay home. Don't worry. I'll be fine."

"Mami, did you really see droplets the colors of the rainbow when that stupid man sneezed his mask off?" asked Irene.

Isabel sighed. "I don't know. It seemed that way at the time. But I won't let any stupid sneezers get anywhere near me this time. I promise you." She simulated a karate chop. "Sneezers beware!"

Irene wasn't sure it was possible to predict who was going to sneeze, but hey, what was important was that her mom was like her mom again. Isabel still spent lots of time in her room having private conversations on the phone, but that was okay. Irene liked to talk to Paola and her other close friend, Carola, in private, too.

Isabel told her daughter that she had found out that they could go bike riding if they wore masks.

"Paola said the police only let people with dogs walk around," said Irene.

"No, the governor gave a new order permitting certain types of outdoor exercise. About time, right?"

"Yeah. Let's take our field glasses."

They had just reached the oceanside park in Isla Verde when Isabel stopped to answer her phone. Irene braked, too, stopped close to her mom, and pulled out her field glasses as though to look for birds. The voice on the other end was not Gladys. It was a man. It didn't sound like her dad, and the way her mom smiled, the soft tone she adopted, wasn't the way she would talk to her dad either. Well, maybe it was the way she talked to him when Irene was little, but not recently.

Tricky

The following week, Isabel told her daughter that she had reconnected with an old friend, a guy she studied in college with. He had stayed in the States many years working in computer programming after graduation, but he had returned home to Puerto Rico just before the Coronavirus outbreak. "He's really nice. You'll like him. His name is David."

Now Irene knew who it was on the phone. The guy really did turn out to be nice. He had salt and pepper hair, dark brown eyes and a beard. He was shorter than her dad, and his voice was not as deep. He brought a present for Irene. It was a book about sea animals.

"Your mom said you already have lots of bird books."

"Yeah. Thanks. Now I can read about manatees. I saw one last year near Rincón."

David was a surfer and he had not only seen lots of manatees, but also whales off the west coast of Puerto Rico.

"How's your online schooling going?" he asked.

"Okay, I guess. Except for math. My other grades are good, but I think I might fail math."

"Oh dear," said Isabel. "I haven't been a good parent at online school. And math isn't my thing. David, do you think you could help her?"

David wore a mask when he visited. He hooked up Irene's small computer to the TV in the living room so that the math teaching videos came to life on the big screen. When she didn't get it, he would kid around about not letting a bunch of naughty little numbers get the better of her, and then provide a much better explanation than the online guy. Irene decided math wasn't such a horrible subject after all. She got a B plus on the final exam, her best grade in math all year.

She was eager to show her dad her grades. On her next visit to his apartment, she got him to open his computer, and put in the password for her school website. She scrolled down to her report card. He was very proud of all her A's and even prouder that she got a B in the subject she hated, math.

The Pinch of the Crab

"Well, I decided that I don't hate math any more. Numbers are not so bad, you just have to understand how they work, you know, how to be as tricky as they are. Don't let the little tricksters trick you, you have to trick them. That's what David says."

Uh oh. Irene had messed up big time.

"Good," said her dad. "I like that way of putting it. Trick the tricksters. But who's this David you're talking about?"

Irene scrolled down further. "Mira, Papi, I got honorable mention for the second best essay on the Great Depression."

"Wonderful! That's my girl. But I asked you a question. Who's David? Your mother and I have an agreement that you are not to see anyone until it's completely safe. Tell me the truth. This is a question of responsible parenting. I have to know."

"David? Oh, that's just my imaginary friend."

"Come on, you're too old for imaginary friends."

"Papi, it's the Coronavirus. I'm super lonely."

Her dad gave her a look that meant he wasn't falling for it.

Irene produced a big smile. "Just kidding. David is the guy in the on-line video program that teaches math. He has this super annoying squeaky voice, but he knows how to explain things."

Strike Three

"Eddie, we have to talk."

My eighteen-year-old son looked up from his bed. When I sat down next to him, I could hear the deep bass beat from his headphones. He removed them from his ears gingerly, so as not to joggle the huge bandage covering the top of his head where they had stitched his scalp back together.

"Whassup, Mom?"

"What on earth gave you the idea to dive head first into the water? At a beach you'd never been to before."

Eddie looked past me, his green eyes fixed on the window, his face deeply tanned. I had taught him how to swim when he was a curly-haired toddler at the beach in Guánica on the Caribbean side of Puerto Rico, where the water is calm, but now he was into surfing the big waves in Rincón.

"I dunno, Mom. I wasn't fully awake yet, I guess. Paco told me to get my ass out of bed, come on, the water's fine and the next thing I knew…"

"There can be hidden rocks and coral at a sandy beach."

"I just wasn't thinking. It was a freak accident."

It had been five days since the doctors at the Emergency Center in Mayagüez saved his life. His father and I hadn't quizzed him until now.

The Pinch of the Crab

"Were you guys drinking the night before?"

Eddie fingered his headphones. "Mom, we had a couple of beers, but I wasn't drunk out of my mind."

"It's not only cracking open your head. Four months ago, you ran my car off the road."

Eddie kept silent. He must have been speeding, because he missed the exit curve off the Expressway and hit a palm tree. Miraculously, he was unhurt, but the car was totaled.

"Something's not right," I said. "You've got to ask yourself why you are taking big risks."

"For God's sake, I'm not suicidal, if that's what you mean." Eddie gave me that sweet smile that made you forgive him on the spot. "I just fucked up... I mean messed up. But Mom, I like being alive. Believe me."

My grandmother always said misfortunes come in threes. Anyone can have one accident. The second one should serve as a warning, but watch out for strike three.

"Look, Eddie, you've had two serious accidents in less than six months. Right before diving in, didn't you have any premonition?"

Eddie admitted feeling he was about to do something dangerous, but went ahead.

"That's got to change," I told him.

My husband Edgardo thought it was all very well to tell Eddie to stop and listen to his own instincts before doing something foolish. "But what teenager will follow that advice if he's with friends who are egging him on? The real problem is the crowd Eddie's hanging out with. Who in hell is this Paco dude Eddie went to Rincón with?"

"Es un buen tipo. He's come over several times to go surfing with Eddie. They met at the University of Puerto Rico."

"What kind of family does he come from?"

"His father is a policeman."

"Dios mío. Nowadays, anybody can get into the University. Children of garbage collectors, policemen, whatever."

"For God's sake. It's a public university. And it's 1997, not 1897."

Edgardo shrugged.

"And besides, Eddie's the grandson of a cabdriver," I added, reminding him that my dad put me and my brother through college driving a taxi in New York.

"Yeah, but you are an English teacher," Edgardo countered. "My point is this Paco dude is a bad influence."

"Paco saved Eddie's life. Drove him immediately to Emergency in Mayagüez."

Edgardo changed his tune the next day when Paco brought Eddie his assignments from the University, so he wouldn't fall behind. Paco looked embarrassed when we thanked him, and said that his buddy Eddie would do the same for him.

A couple of weeks later, the doctor said the wound was healing nicely. By the end of November, Eddie was back to surfing. I know the date because that year it was my turn to cook Thanksgiving dinner. Edgardo's sister Daisy had done it the year before. Most of my family had migrated to New York, but the Rodríguez clan was large enough to pack our apartment tight as a tin of sardines.

The next day I was so tired from all that cooking and cleaning I overslept. Edgardo already had the coffee made. I poured myself a cup, and took some toast out to where Edgardo was reading the newspaper on the balcony.

"Where's Eddie? Still sleeping?"

"Nah. He got up early to go to the beach."

I stood up to look at the little strip of ocean still visible after a new condo was built obstructing our view. The sea wasn't its usual turquoise, but grey green with lots of whitecaps.

"The waves look big," I said.

"Eddie said he wasn't going to surf. He was just going to keep his buddies company."

"Yeah, sure."

Edgardo looked at me over the newspaper. "Dr. Ramos cleared him to go back to normal life."

"I just wish his normal life didn't include surfing."

"He wasn't surfing when he had the accident," Edgardo pointed out.

I didn't bother to argue that it would never have happened if he hadn't gone for a surfing weekend at Rincón. My husband and I had already been over this ground. The bottom line was that it would be sissy to give up a sport because of an accident.

Edgardo put down his newspaper. "How are his grades?"

"I wouldn't know."

"You're his mother. It's your business to know."

I had told Edgardo many times that the wonderful mother and son relationship, that easy understanding we had all during his childhood, had disappeared once he became a teenager. My son used to share *everything* important in his life with me, and now I was lucky if he told me *anything*.

"Why is it my exclusive responsibility?" I asked, switching to English.

Our courtship had been exclusively in Spanish, but whenever I was annoyed, I spoke in English. If the argument escalated into a verbal slugfest, my Brooklyn accent became more pronounced.

"Eddie has always confided in you," said Edgardo, his voice softer now.

"Not anymore."

"And besides you're home more than I am."

"That's just the point," I said. "Nowadays you're never home."

"What's that supposed to mean?"

"He's an adult now. If I push too hard, he talks back. I can't handle Eddie all by myself."

"Amor, for God's sake, you've got to hold the fort," Edgardo gave me one of those smiles that make you forget you were ever mad at him. Like son like father. "I just need a couple of months to be sure I get the second contract. Cut me some slack."

I didn't reply. It was no use. Edgardo's planning firm had landed a contract to do a pilot project on the impact of the new Health Plan on the poor in a single barrio. If his company performed well, they would be in a good position to land the island-wide study. Edgardo saw a second contract as the pot of gold at the end of the rainbow. He dreamed of getting a bigger apartment in one of those luxury high rise condos right on the ocean, complete with maid's room. Eddie would get good grades and we'd send him to the States to get an MBA at Wharton.

I got us both a second cup of coffee. Now there were thunder clouds piling up on the horizon. Sipping his coffee, Edgardo opened the newspaper to the business section, but a cool breeze off the ocean ruffled the pages. It began to rain, a hard slanting rain, followed by lightning and distant rumblings of thunder that became louder as the storm moved in to shore.

Edgardo squashed the flyaway newspaper pages onto his knee. "I have to go look for them."

"I'm sure they have enough sense to get out of the water." But I wasn't sure. Surfers love the big waves kicked up by a storm.

We retreated from the balcony back to the living room. Edgardo began pacing the floor. The electric storm went on and on. He tried Eddie's cell phone number with no luck.

The doorbell rang. I ran to open it. It was Eddie and Paco with body boards.

"¡Dios mío! You guys weren't out in the storm?"

"That's when the waves are best, Mom!"

"¡Brutales!" said Paco, with a big grin.

"But there was lightning. Are you guys out of your minds?"

"Mom, we know what we're doing."

"Mrs. Rodríguez," said Paco, "it's not really dangerous. You count how many seconds between lightning and thunder. More than five seconds, the storm is far out to sea. Less than five, head for the shore."

"Nice to know there's method to your madness," I replied. "Hey, don't go into the house with your feet all sandy."

The Pinch of the Crab

As they bent down to brush off their feet, I noticed a smoky smell clinging to their hair, like a whiff of stale cigarettes mixed with perfume. That sweet smell struck me as odd. Eddie's friends were regular guys.

A week later, Eddie asked me whether Paco could live with us for a couple of weeks. Finals were coming at the University of Puerto Rico and his best friend had nowhere to stay.

"What happened to his parents?"

"His mom went to Newark."

"And his father?"

"He's an asshole."

Finding out what was really going on was like pulling teeth, but Eddie finally told me that Paco's father was living with another woman. The next day, he informed me that everything would be okay. Paco would stay in Barrio Obrero with his grandmother, Doña Marta. "But you know, Mom, Doña Marta needs a job."

"What kind of a job?"

"She was taking care of an old lady in New York. Now she has a couple of cleaning jobs, but only twice a week."

"We already have Olga coming in once a week, and we can't afford more than that," I said. "What's wrong with Paco? Let him get a job."

"He's working at Burger King. But that's not enough."

I told Eddie I would try to help. A few days later he brought Doña Marta to meet me. She was a petite woman with bright eyes and a soft voice. She told me how pleased she was that Paco had found a friend like Eddie at the University. "I knew right away that he was from a good family with good Christian values." She sounded just like my grandmother.

Doña Marta had spent 15 years in Brooklyn only about ten blocks from where I grew up. Once we had swapped memories of the old neighborhood, it wasn't long before she told me her life story. She had only one son, Luis, who had never finished college, as she hoped he would, but finally got a good job on the police force in Puerto Rico and married his pregnant girlfriend, Wendy. At first Doña Marta thought her daughter-in-law was kind of wild, but once Wendy gave birth to Paco and his sister Pilar, she settled down to be a good mother. About a year ago, Wendy got a fulltime office job so that the family could buy their own place. Doña Marta came back from New York to help out.

"I wish I'd stayed in New York."

"You don't get along with your daughter-in-law?"

"It's not that. Wendy's okay."

I waited for her to continue.

"My son didn't do right by his family. You know how Puerto Rican men are," she said, giving me a look that could mean only one thing. Her son had another woman on the side.

"Yeah, and we Puerto Rican women shouldn't put up with it."

"Wendy didn't know," said Doña Marta. "I kept telling her not to worry, he just had to work long hours. God forgive me for lying. Luis's father left me when Luis was only three. I didn't want Paco and Pilar to grow up fatherless."

"What happened when Wendy found out?"

"Wendy has a bad mouth when she's mad. I tried to warn her to be careful, but she told me to get out of the house if I was going to side with that damn puta. When my son came home, she must have let him have it. Luis claims she hit him first. God only knows. I got a call from Paco from the hospital. Wendy's nose was broken. I can't believe my son could do that."

I handed her a Kleenex to wipe the tears.

"She could bring a lawsuit for domestic abuse," I said.

"Wendy left for the States."

I nodded. Domestic violence cases against policemen don't have much chance.

"Wendy took Pilar with her. But she didn't want to take Paco out of college. That's why I have to give him a home here. He can't live with his father and that puta."

The Pinch of the Crab

Doña Marta had made her case. Her son's family had fallen apart, but here she was picking up the pieces, making sure her grandson got through college. My own family had gone through bad times when my mother got so depressed that she could hardly get out of bed. It was my grandmother who came in and kept the household going, making sure I got into college. I was heartbroken when she died of breast cancer, a year after my graduation.

I told Doña Marta I would ask around to see if any of my friends needed help. She embraced me. We had been talking for over an hour. "Dios mío. I've got to be at the dentist in half an hour. Can I drop you somewhere?"

"No, don't worry. My son must already be waiting for me downstairs."

We went down the elevator together. Her son's car was parked outside. He got out and shook hands with me, thanking me for helping his mother out. I had expected a big, burly cop, but this man was slender and soft-spoken.

"Nice condo," he said, looking approvingly at my building.

"It's convenient. You can walk to Pueblo supermarket and there are good schools nearby."

"Yeah. It's a good neighborhood," he said. "Must be worth twice what you paid for it."

I nodded. He was right, even though the ocean view wasn't what it had once been.

"My boss bought an apartment over there," he said pointing to a smaller condo across the street. My ex wanted one in the same building, but I told her it was too pricey."

I looked at my watch and said I had to run.

Doña Marta gave me another hug. Her son extended his hand politely, "Nice to meet you, Mrs. Rodríguez."

Finding a fulltime job for Doña Marta was not going to be easy. Most of my friends did their own housework or had someone in once a week. Then I thought of Cuqui Hernández whose son went to high school with Eddie. Her husband was in construction. They had a big house in Tintillo Hills.

Cuqui said that my call was a Godsend. She was going crazy. Her husband wanted to have this big dinner party for these business guys from the States. Her Dominican housekeeper's grandmother was dying of cancer and the woman had left a week ago. "Just like that! These Dominicans never think of anyone but themselves. After all I've done for her, she could have at least found a substitute."

Jesus Christ! But telling Cuqui that she was the real selfish bitch wouldn't help Paco's grandmother.

"Is this Doña Marta a Dominican?" she asked.

"No, she's from here. Her grandson has a class with Eddie at the University."

"Magnífico."

When I met Cuqui at a party a week later, she said Doña Marta was a find. Without her, all that business entertaining her husband insisted on in the Christmas season would have been impossible. My own holiday social calendar was full. In addition to family festivities, Edgardo wanted me to accompany him to business functions. One day he told me we had to go to this party. The Health Secretary would be there.

"Amor, can you get your hair done?"

Edgardo isn't one of those men who are always telling their wives how to dress. He was really on edge.

"I'll try. But the salons are normally full on Fridays."

I did my hair at home with extra care, and chose a lavender silk evening dress. When Edgardo came home, he was in a better mood.

"Baby, you look good enough to eat. I've got real good news. Our project for the Health Department got an excellent evaluation."

"Wonderful. Now you can stop worrying."

Edgardo told me it was really important to make a good impression on the Health Secretary. We had to leave before Eddie came home, because we couldn't be a minute late for the friggin' party. I would have liked to know what my son's plans were. My husband told me to stop acting like a mother hen. Not fair. He was the one always urging me to keep tabs on our son.

I drank two Cuba Libres, beyond my limit, but it sure did make the small talk flow more easily. The Secretary of Health didn't put in an appearance until after ten. Edgardo was in seventh heaven when he got a chance to chat with him for five minutes. Mission accomplished, time to leave, but Edgardo insisted on staying. We didn't get home until after midnight.

When we came in the door, reggaeton music was coming from Eddie's room.

"Let's go say hi," said Edgardo.

We knocked. No answer. The music was going full blast, but there was no one there.

Edgardo looked at his watch. It was a quarter to one.

"It's early yet," he said.

I yawned. "I just wish I knew where he is."

"Check if there are any calls."

I looked at the phone log and recognized Paco's home number. Doña Marta answered. She hadn't seen Paco all day, but he must be with Eddie. "Don't worry," she told me. "They never get back from Old San Juan before 2 AM."

Edgardo and I waited up for a while, and then went to bed. The telephone rang. I grabbed the receiver. "Hello."

No one answered. I was about to hang up. A small voice that sounded like Eddie said, "It's me, Mom."

"Thank goodness. "Where are you?"

"In jail."

"WHAT?"

"The cops picked us up for smoking pot—Paco and me."

"OH, MY GOD!"

Edgardo sat up and switched on the light. "It's Eddie," I told him. "He's in jail."

"I can't talk long. You've got to get me out!" said Eddie.

Edgardo grabbed the receiver out of my hand. He found out that Eddie was in the jail in Puerto Nuevo, and reassured him we'd get him out. I was crying. Edgardo tried calling his sister Daisy whose husband's brother was a lawyer.

"Fuck, my goddamn hand is shaking."

I dialed for him. It rang forever before Daisy picked up. They would reach her husband's brother Charlie and get back to us. After 15 minutes, she called back. Nothing could be done until morning. Her husband and his brother the lawyer would meet us at the station at eight o'clock.

Edgardo got up and began to get dressed. "Eddie's expecting me. I've got to go to him."

"You won't be able to get him out without a lawyer."

"I can't just sit here doing nothing. Querida, you have no idea what prisons are like in Puerto Rico."

Under ordinary circumstances this would have ticked me off. Just because I grew up in New York, doesn't mean I'm some Anglo fresh off a cruise ship. But forget that.

The telephone rang. It was Doña Marta again. She had gotten a call from Paco, and had called her son to go with her to the police station. "If Luis goes to the station, they won't be mistreated. You know what I mean."

"It's the Puerto Nuevo station. We'll meet you there," I told her.

No answer, just choking noises.

"Doña Marta? Can you hear me?"

"Missie, my son Luis refuses to go. He won't lift a finger for his own son. Must be that stupid puta he's living with. She's jealous of his wife and children. I'm going over to his place right now. Missie Rodríguez, please call Luis and tell him he has to go. Something awful could happen to them."

"But he only met me once," I protested. "Why should he listen to me?"

"He knows what kind of people you and your husband are," said Doña Marta.

The Pinch of the Crab

I wrote down the number. Edgardo didn't want me calling some asshole of a policeman. But if the man can help Eddie, what does it matter if he's an asshole? Edgardo gave in. I dialed the number. A woman answered. I asked to speak to Luis.

"Mire, señora, he's sleeping, and he doesn't like to be waked up in the middle of the night."

"Por favor, es una emergencia. His son and mine are both in jail."

She finally put Luis on the phone. I asked him whether he was aware that Paco was in jail.

"Pendejo. Fucking idiot!"

I gasped.

"Sorry, Ma'am. Pardon my French."

The "French" wasn't what bothered me, it was his fucking attitude.

"It's okay," I said. "We're pretty upset with Eddie, too. But we want to get them out. Bad things could happen to them."

"Serves their smart asses right. If I've told Paco once, I've told him a thousand times. Hold on a minute." Luis got off the phone.

Female voices were screaming. One was saying "We're not gonna pay a cent to get that bastard of a grandson of yours out of jail. Let him rot. You're always talking like he's a saint. He's a goddamn druggie." Then Doña Marta screamed that she would kill the woman if she said one more word about Paco.

Luis intervened, "Shut the hell up. The both of you. Right now. I'm talking on the phone and you two are going to shut up until I'm done."

When Luis came back on, he asked, "Mrs. Rodríguez, what exactly do you want me to do at this time of night?"

"Please go with me and my husband to the police station."

"All right. I'll be at your place in twenty minutes."

Luis was true to his word. In twenty minutes, he showed up with Doña Marta. Probably he didn't want to leave the two women together while he was out. Doña Marta was weeping. Luis told her to cut it out.

"Have you got in touch with a lawyer?" he asked Edgardo.

"Yes, of course."

"Then sit tight until morning. Nothing will happen to them. Let them stew a while. It'll teach them a lesson."

"No, we've got to see Eddie," I interjected. "He has asthma. We've got to be sure he has medicine, just in case."

Luis shook his head and said, "All right, we'll go tonight."

We all stood up.

"Wait a minute," said Luis, looking at Edgardo. "Mr. Rodríguez, you know how it is. I can't take everyone. The comandante will be annoyed. Just you or Mrs. Rodríguez."

Edgardo said he would go.

Doña Marta and I sat down in the living room. Her chest was heaving with the effort of keeping her sobs under control. She knelt on the rug, closed her eyes, and began praying.

"Dear God, save my Paco and his friend Eddie. They made a small mistake, but they are good boys."

She kept her eyes closed for a long time, before pulling herself up on the easy chair.

"Missie Rodríguez, you don't know what policemen are like here. They'd just as soon beat up a couple of kids if they get a chance. Just for the fun of it. And the jails are controlled by gangs. My sister's grandson got arrested. Eighteen years old. Good looking. You don't want to know what they did to him. And the guards just laughed and watched while they held him down."

"Jesus Christ! Stop!" I screamed.

Doña Marta did a complete about face. She assured me her son was a man with influence on the force and nothing would happen to the two young men. Then she asked my permission to make me us both a cup of coffee.

After what seemed like forever, the men returned. They had seen Eddie and Paco. It wasn't possible to bail them out before morning, but they were being held in a temporary holding cell with no other prisoners. No need to worry about them being raped or beaten by hardened criminals. Eddie showed no signs of an asthma attack, but they left the medicine with a guard who promised to check on him. All this was good news, but Luis was doing all the talking. Why wasn't Edgardo saying anything?

"Are you sure they're all right?" I asked.

"Don't worry, Ma'am," said Luis, but Edgardo blurted out, "Eddie has a black eye."

"My God, what did they do to him?"

"Calm down. It was an accident."

"An accident?"

"The police told them to get out of the car," Edgardo explained. "Eddie didn't understand he was supposed to spread his legs and put his hands on the side of the car. They gave him a shove, and he fell against the left side mirror of the car."

"Ma'am, the police are pretty jumpy these days," said Luis. "So many young guys have guns. They didn't mean to hurt him."

I didn't reply. Policemen are like doctors, they stick up for each other, even when the wrong kidney is taken out.

Edgardo assured me that the eye itself wasn't hurt.

We bailed them out early next morning. The probable cause hearing was to be held in two weeks.

Daisy's brother-in-law, Licenciado Carlos Morales, Attorney at Law, aka Charlie, asked to interview the two young men alone. When Edgardo and I went to his office later, Charlie told us Eddie had been driving, and both boys admitted to smoking a couple of joints in the car before being stopped by the police for clipping a red light. The telltale odor of marijuana had tipped the police off. When the car was searched a box was found under the seat. Both young men insisted they knew nothing about the box. Earlier in the evening they had given a ride to some guy named Roberto and one of his buddies. The amount of weed in the box was more than half an ounce, considered possession for personal use. Eddie and Paco could be charged with possession of illegal substances with intent to deal, in other words drug trafficking.

Edgardo asked, "What's the penalty?"

"Ten years."

This news hit me like a swift punch to the stomach. "Oh, my God," I yelled, "it's weed for God's sake, not cocaine."

Charlie shook his head. "In Puerto Rico it doesn't matter. An illicit substance is an illicit substance."

"You mean they could spend ten years in the clunker for smoking a couple of joints?" I asked him.

"That's the way it is. The mafiosos who run the drug trade never get caught, but youngsters who smoke a joint now and then get put in jail."

"Did you talk to the policeman who arrested them?" asked Edgardo.

"Yeah. Agent Irizarry. He asked about your son's eye."

"Nice of him to be concerned."

"He said it was his partner."

"They all say that. Who are they kidding? War on drugs, my ass. Did you read about those seven policemen arrested for marketing the drugs they confiscated?"

The lawyer held up his hand. "Agent Irizarry seems to be straight. He's Pentecostal."

"Shit," said Edgardo.

Charlie turned to me. Probably thought I didn't get the message. "Pentecostals think drugs are sinful," he said. "Sinners have to be punished to bring them back to God."

"By putting them in jail for ten years to be raped and beaten," added Edgardo.

I put my hand over my ears.

"Of course, they are both university students with no previous record. That should help our case," said Charlie. "Is there anything else I should know?"

"Paco's father is a policeman. His name is Luis Figueroa. Paco's grandmother said her son is pretty high ranking," I said.

"I'll check into it," Charlie told me.

The hearing was scheduled for Wednesday. We all went to court, but were informed that the docket was too full and the hearing was postponed for a week. Charlie was pleased because he would have time to meet with Paco's father, Lieutenant Luis Figueroa. It would also give time for the bruising around Eddie's eye to go away so he would look clean-cut.

The night before the rescheduled hearing I didn't sleep at all. I could feel Edgardo tossing and turning beside me. We both got up at five and drank a cup of coffee. When Eddie joined us at breakfast, father and son kept up a normal conversation. I answered in monosyllables. Eddie put his arms around me and said everything would be okay. I retreated to the bathroom to keep from crying in front of them.

It wasn't until we all piled into the car that Eddie stopped talking. The air-conditioning was working, but he was wiping drops of perspiration off his brow. We picked up Paco and Doña Marta on the way. It was only eight thirty when we arrived, but a sign said the parking lot for the Judicial Center in Hato Rey was full. Edgardo muttered "fuck" and started to back the car. A loud honk let him know he had almost crashed into the car behind. After circling for twenty minutes, we parked several blocks away.

The Judicial Center was constructed of massive slabs of concrete, a futuristic version of El Morro fort in Old San Juan that had once housed prisoners in dungeons. We had to wait to go through an electronic monitor. After walking down a long corridor, we took our seats on hard wooden benches along with dozens of other people in the waiting room. Edgardo went to talk to the policeman at the front desk, and found out the case wouldn't be called for another couple of hours. My head was aching. I closed my eyes to shut out the harsh fluorescent lighting. The two boys were talking in low tones. Edgardo glared at them and they kept their mouths shut.

The judge was a stout woman with short gray hair and large spectacles who spoke in a loud voice. Charlie had told us she had a reputation as a no-nonsense judge, who strictly limited the time allotted to each case to keep her docket moving right along.

Strike Three

The policeman who had stopped the car was called to the stand. Up to this time, I had seen no sign of Paco's father, but he entered the chamber while the judge was asking routine questions to determine the officer's name and number of years on the force. He took a seat on the other side of the room without a glance at Paco or at us, his eyes on the policeman.

Officer Irizarry appeared nervous on the stand. First, he said Paco was the driver and then corrected himself to say it was Eddie.

Then Charlie, our lawyer, got to cross examine. "Officer Irizarry, why did you stop the car?"

"They went through a red light."

"If I understand you correctly, you stopped the car for a traffic violation?"

"Yes," said Irizarry.

"And you were just doing a routine spot check for drugs?"

The policeman glanced at Luis who had his eyes fixed on him. "That's right," said Irizarry.

Where was Charlie going with this?

"You had no reason to believe these two young men had drugs on them?' said Charlie. "You didn't see them smoking a joint or anything, did you?"

"No, sir, like I said, a routine spot check."

Now I was beginning to understand. Irizarry had not mentioned the telltale scent of marijuana that he had emphasized when first interviewed by our lawyer.

"Did these two young men, Eddie Rodríguez and Paco Figueroa, offer any resistance?"

"No."

"What was their reaction when you opened the box?"

"Well…"

"Answer the question, Officer," said the judge.

"Let me rephrase," said Charlie. "Did they act surprised?"

I expected the judge to tell our lawyer to stop leading the witness, but maybe I've been watching too many *Law and Order* reruns.

"Yeah," said Irizarry. "They just stared." He pointed to Paco. "That one over there said, "Coño, what's this?'"

Somebody in the courtroom laughed. The judge glared. "Go on."

The policeman continued. "Then the other one said he'd never seen the box before. It didn't belong to them. I asked, how did it get in your car? They told us they'd given some dude a ride."

"Was the dude's name Roberto?"

"Yeah. That's what they said."

"Did you ask them where this guy lives?"

"Lloréns Torres," replied the policeman, naming a housing project in San Juan known as a haven for traffickers. "That's what they told me."

"Did you believe them?"

"I dunno. I see a controlled substance in a car, I arrest whoever's in the car. They sounded pretty sincere, but that's for the courts to decide, sir."

"Let me put in another way, Officer, did you see anything to make you think the box probably belonged to one of these young men?"

"Not really."

The judge told him to step down. She looked disgusted. I suppose she was thinking that sort of wishy-washy testimony was unlikely to get a conviction in court, so why waste the taxpayer's money by continuing the case. She banged the gavel and announced a finding of no probable cause. For a long moment we all just sat there. Eddie wasn't going to jail for the next ten years after all. The judge was calling the next case. We filed out of the courtroom.

Doña Marta was weeping with relief. I hugged Eddie. Edgardo was busy thanking Charlie for his excellent handling of the case. After our lawyer left, Luis strode over and asked whether he could have a word with the two young men.

"Go right ahead," said Edgardo.

"Mami, you stay here," said Luis to Doña Marta. He beckoned to the rest of us to follow him, guiding us to a small room ten feet by ten with one window with bars. It looked like an interrogation room, but was probably for lawyers to meet their clients. There were only two chairs. Luis gestured for Edgardo and me to sit down. The two young men stood against the far wall, arms dangling.

Luis turned to Edgardo. "Mr. Rodríguez, you don't mind if I talk some sense into these two, do you?"

"It's about time they had a reality check," Edgardo replied, allowing the younger man to take charge.

Luis ordered, "Come over here."

Paco and Eddie approached. Luis held himself erect, like a military man, while the two young men slouched, shame-faced before him.

"Listen, and listen hard. You are two lucky sons of a gun. You don't deserve to get off scot-free. If it were up to me…"

"I didn't do nothing," said Paco. "I didn't even know the box was there."

"Oh, so now you're going to say that it was Eddie's box. Well, let me tell you, you arrogant little prick, not only have you brought shame on me, but look what you've done to Mr. and Mrs. Rodríguez. They let you into their house, and you corrupted their only son, you son of a bitch."

"I never did that."

Luis grabbed his son's shirt.

I stood up. "Mr. Figueroa, please."

Ignoring me, he twisted Paco's collar until it tightened around his neck. "Dímelo otra vez, you goddamn liar."

"I'm not a liar," Now that he was standing up straight Paco looked taller than his father. "I'm telling the truth."

"Un momento, are you talking back to me?" Luis didn't raise his voice. He didn't have to.

Paco flinched, but said nothing.

"Hijo de puta, answer me."

The Pinch of the Crab

Paco glowered at his father. "You're the one living with a whore."

The next instant Paco was on the floor felled by a swift blow to the side of the head. Luis kicked him in the ribs.

"Me has faltado el respeto. Do you think you can get away with it?"

Paco was silent.

"Do you want more? Answer me."

Silence. Luis landed several vicious kicks in quick succession.

Eddie screamed, "Stop, Paco's telling the truth."

Luis paused. His face was flushed and he was breathing hard.

"Escúchame, Paco never took drugs before he met me. I'm the one who got the weed." Eddie was sobbing loudly. "Please, Mr. Figueroa, it's not his fault."

Luis shrugged. "You didn't force him to smoke the goddamn weed, did you?"

Eddie didn't answer.

"I'm going to teach him not to disrespect his father," said Luis.

"I think he's learned his lesson, Mr. Figueroa," said Edgardo, stepping forward.

Luis shook his head. "I don't care what he's learned. He is going to apologize to his father." Luis aimed another kick at his son. "Get up."

Paco got to his feet slowly, his face contorted. He doubled his fists and took a step toward his father. I gasped. Luis touched the gun in his holster.

Paco's shoulders slouched and he retreated. "Sorry, Papi."

Whew! I let my breath out slowly. The danger was over, but it was hard to say whether Paco had uttered those two words of apology in a submissive whisper or a defiant hiss.

"Stand up straight."

Although Luis was addressing Paco, Eddie also stood at attention. The tears were still running down his cheeks.

Luis continued, "I hope you've both learned your lesson. Next time you'll get ten years. I won't lift a finger for either of you. Just wait and see what the other inmates do to you. You two have been coddled and spoiled.

Strike Three

You want to be held down by four men while another one sticks it up yours? And if you don't get arrested, you'll get killed on the street. You guys think you've got street smarts. Let me tell you, you don't know nothing, nothin' at all. So, you think Roberto is your friend? Gets your weed for you. Do you guys have any idea who he works for? If you're a day late to pay, he'd just as soon kill you for five hundred dollars, nah, fifty, or just for fun, show the boss he's a real macho man, yeah, why not practice on a couple of pendejos—fuckin' idiots like you two who have no idea what they're doing."

"As for you," he turned to Eddie, "you should have more respect for your parents. After all they've given you, is this the way you repay them?"

"I'm sorry, sir."

Silence.

Finally, Luis turned to me and said, "Sorry, Ma'am, I try not to use bad language in front of ladies, but you'll pardon me for telling it like it is."

I nodded, speechless.

Edgardo said to Eddie, "I hope you listened to Mr. Figueroa carefully. He knows what he's talking about."

"Sí, Papi."

Doña Marta was waiting for us in the hallway. Luis left without saying anything to her. She scanned Paco's face and then asked me whether everything was all right. I nodded my head, not trusting myself to speak. Edgardo said he would drop her and her grandson off. We walked to the car in silence. Edgardo gestured to Eddie to sit up front with him. The rest of us crowded into the back.

I was seated at the right, Dona Marta in the middle, and Paco sat motionless staring out the left rear window. When he wiped his right eye with his shirt, I noticed it was swollen and puffy.

Edgardo said, "Our lawyer did a great job."

"Charlie was good," I replied, "but I'm not sure that it was his legal skill. I think Paco's father got them off."

Paco turned his head and said in a loud voice, "NO! THAT'S NOT TRUE!"

At first, I didn't understand what he was talking about, but his tone surprised me, because he had always been soft-spoken and respectful.

"THAT SON OF A BITCH HAD NOTHING TO DO WITH IT! THE LAWYER GOT US OFF!"

"Paco," said Dona Marta, "watch your manners. Of course, it was the lawyer, but I'm sure your father did his best."

"Papi get me off? Are you out of your mind? That motherfucker'd sooner see me dead, and you dead and my mother dead and my sister. Everyone but that goddamn puta. If he touches my mother again, I'll kill him!"

Dona Marta patted his arm, but he pushed her away and resumed staring out the window, muttering goddamn motherfucker, goddamn motherfucker.

Edgardo didn't tell him to watch his language. He didn't even turn around. Edgardo usually drives with only one hand on the steering wheel, spinning it around like a teenager, but now I could see his two hands clenching the wheel in the ten and two o'clock positions, like they teach you in driving school. The atmosphere in the car was charged, as though an electric current was whirling, waiting to strike. A drop of moisture on my arm told me Doña Marta was weeping silently. Mercifully, we were close to her apartment.

Edgardo pulled over to the curb. Paco flung the door open without looking to see whether a car was coming. He got out, wincing with pain, and walked into the building without a word.

I had to get out first to let Doña Marta pass. While sliding over she thanked Edgardo, "It was very good of you Mr. Rodríguez to tell your lawyer to help Paco. We will always be grateful." She embraced me at curbside, and told me between sobs that I was an angel who had saved Paco's life.

After we got home, I cleared away the dirty breakfast dishes still on the dining table. I filled the sink with water and suds, washed them, and then dried my tears on a clean dishtowel, before wiping the dishes. Once

Strike Three

they were put away, I made a simple lunch of ham and cheese sandwiches. Edgardo and I ate hungrily, but Eddie only took a few bites before asking whether he could be excused.

"Espera un momento," said Edgardo. "Not so fast. There are a few things we have to talk about. We can't just pretend nothing happened and go on with our lives."

Eddie sat back down. "Papi, I know I fucked up big time. But things are going to be different from now on. I promise you."

"That's what you said when you cracked open your head in Rincón," I said.

"Mom, I listened to you. I haven't had any more accidents." Eddie was smiling at me.

I brought my fist down hard on the table. "GODDAMN IT! Don't pretend you don't see the connection. I was talking about going ahead and doing something when you know it's dangerous. You don't have to be a genius to know that lighting up a joint right in the middle of Condado and then driving through a fucking red light is risky as hell. And tell me where do you get the weed? Do you go to a drug punto? Maybe getting arrested is not enough of a goddamn thrill. Next time you'll get yourself shot."

"Mom, Roberto always delivered. I've never gone to a punto, and I never will. I'm giving up the stuff."

The anger drained out of me and I began to cry. Eddie had been the sort of kid who never forgot to take his UNICEF bag trick or treating at Halloween. Good God, what had gone wrong?

Eddie begged me to please stop. He was going to show me that things were different now.

"You should have thought about what it would do to your mother before," said his father.

Once I calmed down, Edgardo said it was time to establish some ground rules for the future. Eddie was to work at his father's office whenever he didn't have class, stay home at night, and concentrate on pulling up his grades. He would be grounded completely for two months, and if his grades improved, he would be allowed to go out once a week with a strict curfew.

Eddie looked glum, but all he said was, "I guess I deserve this." A few minutes later, he again asked whether he could be excused.

"Not so fast," said Edgardo. "That crowd you were hanging around with. You're not to see any of them. No potheads. Got that straight?"

"Yes, Papi,"

"That applies to Paco."

"Why Paco?"

"Because he's a bad influence."

"No, he's not. Paco es un tipo muy decente."

"Mira, Eddie, I understand why you lied to protect him. I didn't want him to be beaten up by his father either."

"Papi, I was telling the truth. Roberto is *my* connection. I got Paco into it."

"Look, Eddie, you can't be so idealistic. Stop trying to be a super hero. This Figueroa guy could be dangerous. If he blames you for getting his son into drugs, he could come after you."

"Papi, that's not going to happen."

Yeah, sure. Eddie was always sure nothing bad was going to happen, and he was messing up everything, not only for himself but for all of us. Edgardo was right. The friendship with Paco had to end. Sure, once upon a time I myself had defended Paco and helped his grandmother get a job, but after seeing Officer Figueroa in action, I would be happy to never see any of them again. The whole family was a fucking nightmare.

"What makes you so damn sure you know what a guy like Figueroa is going to do?" I asked. "Tell me."

Eddie shrugged and stood up.

"Hey, not so fast, sit down, YOU LISTEN TO ME," I screamed. "Figueroa is a sadistic bastard, and the way Paco talked in the car, he's not much better. LOW CLASS PEOPLE, THAT'S WHAT THEY ARE. What's wrong with you? Can't you understand you have to stay away from them?"

Eddie turned and went down the hall toward his room. The door slammed, and then there were scuffing noises, like someone kicking things or opening and shutting drawers. Edgardo and I looked at each other. We had thought Eddie accepted the new ground rules, but we were obviously wrong. The crisis wasn't over. Eddie must be packing up to leave home. The ground rules we had announced would have been fine if he was still fourteen, but he was already eighteen, an adult. What if he came out and told us to shove our fucking rules you know where?

Eddie strode back into the living room. He stood there looking at us, tapping his foot on the floor.

Edgardo said softly, "Hijo, what's on your mind?"

"Look, I fucked up. No argument. But you're wrong about one thing. I wasn't trying to be a super hero in that room in the courthouse. If Paco hadn't been in Rincón I would be dead and buried. The least I could do was to tell his father the truth. Paco got into weed because of me. What was I supposed to do, keep quiet to cover my back, and just stand there watching while that bastard Figueroa put Paco in the hospital? Is that the kind of man you want me to be? A FUCKING SUPER ASSHOLE?"

Internal Injuries

When Cuqui called and invited me to lunch, I claimed to be busy. She wasn't one of my favorite people. The last day of third grade, my son Eddie had come home crying his eyes out, because he wasn't invited to her son's birthday. He was the only boy in the class left out. I should have stuck to my guns, but I let my husband Edgardo persuade me that holding a grudge about something that happened ten years ago was silly.

Although our son had already graduated from Saint John's School, the number one prep academy on the island, Edgardo must have thought the lunch invitation meant I was finally being accepted by the mothers that matter. That sort of thing meant a lot to him. His parents ran a colmado, a mom and pop grocery, on the other side of the island, and Edgardo was the first in the family to go to college. Besides, Cuqui was married to a man who was a long time buddy of Governor Ramos, the newly elected pro-statehood governor of Puerto Rico. Edgardo believed in making contacts.

A couple of hours later, I called Cuqui back and said I would be free tomorrow after all. We arranged to meet at the Patisserie on Ashford Avenue, walking distance from my apartment on San Jorge.

On the way to the restaurant, I crossed over to Parque de los Indios on Ashford Avenue, and stood several moments watching the ocean. A surfer

The Pinch of the Crab

got wiped out by a huge curling wave. I waited anxiously until his head bobbed up and he got back on his board to head out again. A glance at my watch told me I was ten minutes late.

Before entering the Patisserie, I caught sight of Cuqui with two young women at a window table, one of whom was her daughter Cristina. She introduced me to Ashley, Cristina's roommate from Swarthmore, who was spending Easter vacation with them.

Cuqui had on a bright, flowered silk blouse and she wore large gold earrings, with multiple loops and diamonds, the kind that make your ears ache. The two young women, both fashionably thin, wore muted earth tones and tasteful single band gold necklaces. I was telling Ashley about the best beaches on the island, when Cuqui summoned the waitress in a loud voice and ordered a bottle of wine.

I said it was too early in the day for me, but she ordered a glass for each of us anyway. The wine went straight to my bladder. When I returned from the bathroom, and took my seat, our croissant sandwiches had already been served, and Cristina was giggling about how Marcos, one of her former classmates from Saint John's, had been flirting with Ashley at a party the night before.

"Marcos turned out to be a real good-looking guy," said Cuqui.

Fair-skinned Ashley flushed bright red.

"Watch out!" Cristina told her friend. "He's a real player!"

"What do you mean?" asked Cuqui.

"A mujeriego," I translated.

"He seemed very sincere and straightforward," said Ashley, blushing again.

"Ella no sabe cómo son los hombres puertorriqueños," said Cuqui, shaking her head.

"Mom's saying you don't know how what Puerto Rican men are like," said Cristina.

Ashley smiled. "Not just Puerto Rican men. You can't be too trusting of *any* man."

"Yeah," said Cuqui. "You have to keep your eyes open."

I wondered why she was looking at me.

"Un momento," I said, "let's not give Ashley the wrong idea. There are plenty of decent Puerto Rican men."

"Maggie should know," Cuqui replied, pointing to me. "She's been married to the same one forever."

The two young women declined to eat dessert, and left soon after in Ashley's rental car. Cuqui ordered coffee for the two of us. Then she asked me whether I'd heard that her son Iván had been named Housing Secretary.

"Edgardo told me about it," I said. "Give Iván our congratulations."

"Thanks. By the way, how is Edgardo? I haven't spoken to him since the big fund raiser."

Cuqui was talking about the thousand dollar a plate dinner for Governor Ramos we had both attended six months ago. I remembered telling Edgardo I wasn't going. My father had driven a taxi to put me through college, and I wasn't about to give all that money away to some goddamn politician. But Edgardo pointed out that it was hardly the time to be stingy when his consulting firm was bidding for a half-a-million-dollar study of the new health card for the poor.

I told Cuqui that Edgardo was very busy nowadays with a new contract with the Health Department. "In the consulting business, it's either feast or famine," I said. "We hardly see him."

"I saw him a week ago, in Zipperle's, but I don't think he saw me," said Cuqui. "Do you remember the name of the new Assistant Secretary of Health? She made a late entrance at the Governor's dinner. Young, good-looking blonde?"

"You mean Claudia Meléndez?"

"You have a good memory," said Cuqui, giving me a smile. "That's who Edgardo was with at Zipperle's."

"Edgardo has lunch with the people at the Health Department all the time," I said and looked her straight in the eye.

"It was dinner time. About eight thirty," Cuqui replied.

The Pinch of the Crab

I couldn't think of anything to say. I had known Cuqui for many years, but she had never invited me for lunch before. She knew I was born and brought up in Brooklyn. Up to this point, I had assumed the idea was to invite someone to lunch who spoke good English while entertaining Ashley, but it looked like there was another motive.

The waitress came and asked if we wanted anything more.

"Just the check," I said.

Cuqui said that her friend Gloria told her just last week that Claudia went to the same plastic surgeon she did, a man known for working wonders.

By this time, we had exited the restaurant. I politely returned Cuqui's kiss on the cheek. While she waited for the valet to bring her car, I started for home on foot. As I got to the corner of Ashford and San Jorge, it started to drizzle. A loud honk made me realize I was crossing on red.

When I got home, I made myself another cup of coffee. The words "around eight thirty at night" not only rang in my ears, they rammed into my stomach and turned the food I had eaten into a hard lump. The second coffee only made it worse. A wave of nausea sent me to the bathroom. When I finished throwing up, I felt like my first mother's milk had come up, or would have if I'd been breast fed.

I lay down. The lump in my stomach had been replaced by a hollow emptiness. I started dialing Edgardo's private office number, but stopped midway when I remembered he had taken our son Eddie to his office party to celebrate the submission of the first report on the health card project. What was I going to say to him? I needed to get my head straight first. Maybe Cuqui was making up a story to get back at me. But what for? On the other hand, why jump to conclusions? Just because my husband had dinner with Claudia didn't mean he was having an affair.

When father and son got home around seven, I had enough self-control not to bring it up in front of Eddie. Luckily, the guys had eaten too much at the office party to be hungry, and I didn't have to sit through a family dinner. We all three watched TV until Eddie's friends came to pick him up.

"He's a great help at the office," Edgardo said after Eddie left.

I nodded. I was the one who had suggested a part-time job would be good for our son, keep him out of trouble.

"You're awful quiet," said Edgardo. "How was the lunch with Cuqui?"

I muted the sound on the TV. "Strange."

"Come on Maggie, it can't have been that bad."

"What do you want first?" I asked, my voice neutral. "The good news or the bad news?"

"The good news, baby."

"Cuqui said you should give her son a call. I guess there might be some possibility of consulting for the Housing Department."

"Good work, sweetie. Now what's the bad?"

"She's an awful gossip."

Edgardo shrugged. "Okay, so who did she give you the low down on?"

"You."

"What do you mean?"

I told him.

"Maggie, sweetheart, don't tell me that woman worried you. What a witch! She's just trying to get to you. My relationship with Claudia Meléndez is strictly professional. You have to wine and dine them."

"But did you take her to dinner?"

Edgardo hesitated. "Just lunch, I think. He wrinkled his brow as though trying to remember. "Maybe dinner once. Really, it's not important."

"I just wish you told me before someone else did."

"Oye, mi amor, I'm flattered you think I'm still attractive to a young woman like Claudia, but I swear nothing is going on. Negra, I love you."

I began to cry hard. Edgardo comforted me, assuring me that he loved me as much now as the day he proposed. He treasured me and the family we built together. All those resolutions to keep calm, judge with my head not my heart, went flying out the window. We ended up making love like teenagers.

The Pinch of the Crab

I awoke to the first gray light of approaching dawn. Edgardo was snoring by my side. I ran my hand over one breast, cupping it in my hand. The solidity of my body reassured me the lovemaking was real, and I drifted back to sleep. When I awoke, Edgardo already had coffee made. We had a leisurely breakfast before he left for the office.

All day I was like a surfer riding a frothy wave of reconciliation, until Edgardo called me at about four saying he would be late. He had to have a quick drink with Ricky Colorado, the head of the research section of the health insurer Triple S.

"I'll just be an hour late. We'll go out for dinner."

My husband was trying to reassure me. But the phone call made me uneasy. The snapshot of Edgardo swearing his undying love for me was replaced in my head by a man wrinkling his brow, trying to remember whether he had taken Claudia to dinner. What man wouldn't remember? Fucking liar!

I spent the next three days riding a seesaw, up one moment and down the next. I looked forward to the spring vacation ending, hoping that getting back to teaching would steady me. A crisis with the best student in my high school English class, a girl of sixteen, kept my mind off my own problems for a week. But when I finally got Social Services to intervene with her abusive stepfather, my own situation began eating me again.

The feeling of not having my feet firmly placed on the ground didn't go away as summer approached. After that one night of passionate sex, I just went through the motions. The momentary flame inspired by jealousy was replaced by the dull deadening ache of distrust. I needed to talk to someone.

I couldn't put my sister-in-law Daisy on the spot by telling her my suspicions. My other close friend Lola had stayed with her husband after finding him in bed with her younger sister, and was still in therapy.

Then I remembered my American friend Andrea. She had come to Puerto Rico with her husband who worked for Pfizer. By the time the marriage broke up, Andrea had fallen in love with the island. She was into sun worship, yoga and spiritual healing through massage. I called her, and she asked me to lunch at the new "in" place for vegetarians. I'm not much for hummus and bean sprout sandwiches, or carrot juice for that matter, but I needed to talk.

I was expecting Andrea to tell me to take a stand, not let my husband get away with it. After all she had taken a stand with her husband Phil whom she called the Pfizer shmuck. But a string of broken romances after her divorce had taken their toll. She advised me not to take any sudden action.

"Edgardo isn't at all like Phil," she insisted, "and you have to think about your son. Besides, there's no proof of anything, even if you assume he did go to dinner with her. You're letting that bitchy Cuqui woman mess with your head. Why trust her more than your husband?"

"I just can't seem to get it out of my head."

"I see. Cuqui really got to you. You know what my friend Connie did when her husband's ex put the evil eye on her? She consulted an Espiritista. Now Connie is just fine, moving forward with her life. You should try it."

I couldn't quite picture Cuqui sticking pins into a doll. Even she must have something better to do with her time. Still, by the end of the lunch with Andrea I was feeling much better. It was one thing to tell myself there was no reason to trust Cuqui more than my husband. A weak excuse of a woman frightened to lose her marriage. But when an outsider like Andrea made the same argument, it made a lot of sense.

Edgardo did his part to help me get over my suspicions. He was working hard on the health project, but he rarely stayed late, and he called me at least once a day to just chat about how the day was going. Neither of us mentioned Claudia Meléndez again.

By summer's end, I thought we were back into our old groove, until I noticed Edgardo was obsessed with the news. We had always subscribed to the *San Juan Star* for me, as well as *El Nuevo Día* for him, but Edgardo added a third paper, *El Vocero*. He read all of them carefully, and then he would urge me to join him in the TV room to watch the late-night local news.

One evening, the newscast on channel two said the Federal Justice Department was investigating the use of funds for AIDS patients at the San Juan AIDS Institute. They were interviewing Dr. Emilio Orsini, the head of the Institute, a distinguished gent with white hair who solemnly assured the camera that the investigation was pro forma. The Institute was late providing the financial paperwork, because they had been too busy working on a new program geared to the homeless who walk the streets of San Juan.

When the ads came on, I asked, "What was that all about? That Orsini guy sure doesn't look like a crook. His face is kinda familiar."

"Yeah," said Edgardo. "He was at the thousand dollar a plate dinner. He's an honest and dedicated man."

"I hope so. They were talking about taking funds from the AIDS Institute. Just imagine. Stealing from the dying."

Finally, the ads were over. The pretty TV reporter was interviewing Elí Carmona, the Independence Party leader, who was promising to push for a full investigation in the legislature.

"Interesting, I said. "He's an independentista, but he seems happy to back up the Feds."

"Maggie, you don't understand the way things work in Puerto Rico. Anything to get Governor Ramos. It's all politics."

It annoyed me when Edgardo lectured me on how things work in Puerto Rico as though being born in Brooklyn meant I was any less Boricua than he was.

"Carmona sounded sincere," I insisted. "He looked disgusted about a scheme to rob the sick, like any decent person would be."

Edgardo changed the subject. "What worries me is that a full-blown investigation of the AIDS Institute could spill over."

"Spill over?"

"Into investigation of other health contracts."

This conversation worried me, but when I broached the subject the next day, Edgardo told me not to be silly.

"Don't worry sweetheart, we do everything by the book."

I wasn't completely reassured. Edgardo often looked preoccupied, his mind far away. Most nights, he hardly participated in the conversation at the dinner table. Every question I asked him had to be repeated. Even Eddie noticed and remarked to me that Papi is really spaced out.

Every once in a while, Edgardo would come in from outer space, and lay down the law, or try to. That's what happened when I started talking about a teacher from Vieques who had come to talk to my school about the bombing close to populated areas, and the testing of dangerous chemicals like napalm on the small offshore island.

"He moved to Vieques twenty years ago and his wife and son both have cancer," I said. "The poor guy had to choke back tears in the middle of his talk."

Edgardo acted like he hadn't heard what I said, but my son was listening intently.

"Yeah. The cancer rate is like twice as high in Vieques as the rest of Puerto Rico," said Eddie. "Me and Carlos and some other guys from the University are going on the march this Sunday."

Edgardo, who had taken no part in the conversation so far, asked, "What march?"

"Protesting what the Navy's doing to Vieques. We're marching to Old San Juan," Eddie replied.

"Oh no, you're not. It's a bunch of radicals trying to make sure Puerto Rico never becomes a state."

"But Papi, we're American citizens with the right to protest what the government is doing."

The discussion got hot and heavy. Eddie's main point was that he was over eighteen and had the right to make up his own mind about participating in a peaceful protest march. Edgardo countered that everyone in the family should think twice about doing anything that might endanger his contracts with the government. After all, we were living the good life because of his business.

After Eddie left the table and went to his room, slamming the door behind him, Edgardo accused me of egging him on to defy his father.

"Bottom line is you've got to stop him from going on the march," he told me.

"What if we forbid him and he goes anyway?" I said.

"Then let him move out and pay the bills," said Edgardo.

I was surprised. Edgardo is usually the one reminding me that we can no longer treat Eddie like a child, telling me to get hold of my temper, reason with him. My husband was talking like a different man, not the conscientious father who always put his son first.

"It's a good cause," I told him. "We should be happy Eddie cares about what's happening to other people. Most of the kids in my high school classes don't give a shit about what's happening in Vieques or anywhere else. All they want to do is party, not just beer, let me tell you."

"Maggie, for God's sake you don't understand anything."

I was about to say that Edgardo was the one being unreasonable, but when he slammed his beer can down on the coffee table, I held my tongue.

He rubbed his temples for a moment and said: "My head hurts. This family gives me a fucking headache."

Edgardo wasn't one of those guys who used the f-word all the time, at least not in front of me. He was always telling me to clean up my own language, act like a lady. Something had gone very wrong.

"I'll get you some Tylenol."

When I came back with two extra strength pills, Edgardo was slumped forward in his chair, his shoulders trembling. He wiped his eyes with the back of his hand.

"What is it?"

"Where's Eddie?"

"Still in his room."

"I'm in trouble, Maggie."

He handed me the glass of water after swallowing the pills, and told me that the Feds had started investigating political contributions made by Health Department contractors.

"But honey, I don't think going to a $1000 a plate dinner for the Governor would be considered a bribe."

Edgardo shook his head. "I made a much larger contribution. I was just trying to get my company considered on its merits. Like an entrance fee to a contest. If you don't pay, you're not in the running."

"What kind of entrance fee?

"A lot."

"For God's sake, how much?"

"Twenty-five thousand."

I gasped. "What? You gave twenty-five thousand to the Ramos campaign?"

"I knew you wouldn't understand."

"That's our family savings, not yours alone."

"I wasn't thinking only about myself. It was an investment for you and Eddie, the ticket to our future prosperity."

I just stood there, the half-filled glass of water still in my hand, mad as hell. The son of a bitch had taken out twenty-five thousand from our savings without even consulting me. But was he in danger of being charged with anything? Edgardo was scaring the shit out of me. My legs felt like rubber. I sat back down on the sofa and put the glass down on the coffee table. It teetered and almost toppled over.

"They could accuse you of bribery. You could go to jail."

Edgardo reached for my hand. "Maggie, believe me. It wasn't a bribe. I'm proud of making a donation for a good cause. Statehood. Dignity for all Puerto Ricans."

"But would a jury buy that?"

Edgardo slumped back into his chair, like a child whose birthday balloon had been pricked.

The Pinch of the Crab

"You know me, Maggie. I would never try to bribe anyone. I just wanted to level the playing field. But you're right. People might come to the wrong conclusions. I went to see a lawyer."

"What did he say?"

"He's making inquiries. It all depends on who's talking to the FBI. I have another appointment tomorrow. You have to come with me."

"Jesus Christ, Edgardo," I said, trying to keep my voice steady. "How could you do this to us?"

The appointment was for the next day at two in the afternoon at the lawyer's office on Justo Street in Old San Juan. The building had an old-fashioned façade, round columns at the entrance. Inside it had a black and white checkered floor and modern furnishings. We were directed to the third floor occupied by the offices of Álvarez, Dalmau and Petersen. After about twenty minutes, Licenciado Raúl Álvarez, a handsome man with gray hair and a patrician nose, came out. He clapped Edgardo on the back, and said how pleased he was to meet me, while ushering us into his office. You could see a lovely view of San Juan Bay through the picture window.

The first five minutes were spent in small talk. It turned out that Licenciado Álvarez had been two classes ahead of Edgardo at San Ignacio, the school my husband always said not only gave him a scholarship but a start in life.

"It's a small world, isn't it?" said Edgardo. The chatter of the two men about mutual friends reminded me that I was an outsider in the cozy world of people who matter on the island.

Mr. Álvarez glanced at his gold watch and said, "We had better get down to business." He opened a file, stared down at it and drummed his fingers on the table, as though searching for the right words.

"Mrs. Rodríguez, has your husband explained to you why he sought legal advice?"

"Yes."

Edgardo who had been staring at his shoes, his shoulders hunched, looked up, "I explained that I made a large political donation that could be... misinterpreted."

Internal Injuries

The lawyer nodded. "I have good news." He smiled at us both. "The Re-election Committee has no record of a donation from Edgardo Rodríguez."

Edgardo sat up straight. "That's wonderful. Then there's nothing to worry about."

"Not so fast," said the lawyer.

He was right about taking it slow. My head was whirling. If no money was donated to the Committee, where in hell was the twenty-five thousand?

"The Feds have been asking questions," said the lawyer. "They'll be talking to Miss Claudia Meléndez next week."

My stomach muscles tightened. "What does she have to do with it?"

The lawyer opened his mouth, exchanged a glance with Edgardo, and kept silent.

"I gave the money to Claudia," said Edgardo. "To be on the safe side."

I hadn't forgotten my suspicions about Claudia, but what he seemed to be saying was that she was the courier to the Committee.

"It might not be safe," said Álvarez in a low voice. "A large gift to Miss Meléndez doesn't look good given the fact that she was Assistant Secretary of Health. It could have an appearance of impropriety."

My head was spinning. "Impropriety?"

"An effort to secure her influence to get the health card contract."

"You mean bribery?"

The lawyer shook his head as though pained by the word. "Mrs. Rodríguez, you and I both know your husband is an honest man."

"Claudia had nothing to do with the committee that selected the firm for my contract," Edgardo said.

"Good point," said the lawyer. "But the Feds might still be interested in a substantial gift made to the second in command in the agency. Did you give her a check?"

"The first five thousand. After that, I delivered cash".

This was beginning to resemble the plot of a Grade B mafia movie.

"Jesus Christ, Edgardo," I said.

The Pinch of the Crab

Licenciado Álvarez turned to me. "Mrs. Rodríguez, believe me, I understand your concern."

"No, you can't possibly understand," I retorted, struggling not to break down. "For you, it's all in a day's work, but it's the good name of my family."

"Sometimes things appear worse than they seem," the lawyer said in a soothing voice. "Miss Meléndez's lawyer is my wife's cousin. Of course, I didn't discuss your husband's case with him directly. But he did tell me that she is the single mother with one child—an autistic boy of five. You know the schools here on the island don't offer adequate services. Friends have helped her with the expenses of a child psychologist and special schooling."

"You mean Edgardo helped her."

The lawyer nodded.

"Twenty-five thousand for a woman he just met?"

"The check in her name was only for five thousand," Edgardo pointed out.

"But your wife is quite right. Even if the amount is small, the Feds are bound to question why you took on the role of Good Samaritan."

Edgardo changed color. His eyes met mine for a brief second and then he looked out the window at San Juan Bay.

"The Feds are not the only ones who want to know," I said.

No one said anything. Through the airtight window I could hear the muffled shouts of young people and the distant rumble of cars from the street below.

Finally, the lawyer said, "Mrs. Rodríguez, I don't think I have to tell you that your husband is in a dangerous position. Appearances could be against him unless we all pull together. If Claudia reveals anything to the Feds, we will have to address the question of why your husband donated money for the boy's education. The most logical explanation would be what we call a sentimental relationship. Of course, there was none, but…"

Internal Injuries

From the beginning the lawyer had been the perfect gentleman, a concerned friend offering a helping hand. But the web he was spinning was not to save me as Charlotte the spider had rescued Wilbur in the first book that I read by myself. No, he was winding sticky strands round and round my body to make sure I would do nothing against Edgardo. If I didn't say something quick, the gooey stuff would reach my tongue.

"You mean adultery is not a crime, but bribery is?"

Mr. Álvarez frowned. I had broken the rules.

"I am sure your husband had no intention of influencing the contractual process," he said slowly, enunciating each syllable.

"May I assume," I replied, imitating his precise way of speaking, "that you are equally sure that my husband didn't fuck Claudia Meléndez?"

The lawyer muttered something about giving us privacy and excused himself. He walked hurriedly around Edgardo's chair, not mine, to get to the door, tripping on the throw rug in his anxiety to exit.

Once the door closed, Edgardo leaned over and said, "Maggie, sweetheart I'm terribly sorry. I've done some stupid things, but believe me there was never anything between me and Claudia."

"Stop it! I screamed. "You're a goddamn liar. Do you think I'm an idiot?"

"Please, lower your voice. I know this is stressful, but you're making us look bad. Everyone in the building can hear."

I got up from my chair and started to walk toward the door.

"Maggie, I made a terrible mistake. Please let me explain."

"What's to explain? You betrayed your marriage for a goddamn whore who's a thief besides."

Edgardo sighed.

"Where's the twenty-five thousand? Cuqui knows Claudia because they go to the same plastic surgeon. A boob job here and a bit of botox there wouldn't leave much for tutoring, would it? The bit about the autistic son is a sob story if I ever heard one."

The Pinch of the Crab

"Maggie, please, she really does have an autistic child. I'm sure she'll give back the money. But I can't ask her for it. Álvarez says under no circumstances am I to contact her."

"I suppose that's why it's over."

"No, it was over months ago. Maggie, believe me, I love you. It was a stupid midlife crisis."

"That line won't work. Not with me."

"I was flattered when she began asking me for advice about the kid. Like I was her big brother, and then before I knew what was happening…"

"Shut up," I screamed, my hands covering my ears.

"Maggie, please, we've been together for over twenty years."

"It's over," I said.

"Don't do anything hasty. God, Álvarez will be back any moment. Sweetheart, you're in no condition to talk to him."

"You're right about that," I said. "Give me the keys."

"I'll only be with the lawyer a few minutes. Get the car from the parking garage and pick me up."

I took the keys, and walked out the door. Before slamming it hard behind me, I turned to say, "You can find your own fucking way home."

I ran down the stairs rather than taking the elevator. It wasn't until I was on the street that I lost control and began to sob. I couldn't remember on which floor of the Doña Fela parking we had put the damn car. While I was searching my purse for money for a taxi, I remembered it was Edgardo's BMW, not my Toyota.

While driving home I got stuck in traffic on Ashford Avenue. It was about three o'clock when all the mothers pick up their children at Saint John's or Robinson School. I leaned my head against the steering wheel. When I opened my eyes, the light had turned green. I pressed the gas too hard and crashed right into a large black SUV in front of me. The driver, a middle-aged man, came out yelling about stupid women drivers, but he calmed down when he saw only his bumper was dented, while the whole front of my BMW had caved in. By this time, I was crying again. The man asked whether I was hurt. I said no, I'd just had a really shitty day.

By some miracle the BMW started, but every couple of seconds there was a horrible clackety clack, followed by a grinding noise. I just hoped the axle wouldn't break in two. Somehow, I got the car into our covered garage. It was a relief when the door closed and I could no longer see the damage. In spite of everything, I dreaded the moment that Edgardo would set eyes on the wreck.

Thank God, Eddie wasn't home. I collapsed on the bed. There was pressure on my chest, and then in the bones of my head, and my mouth twisted into a grimace. Sobs were forcing their way up but finding no exit, because I couldn't weep. When the tears finally came, I could hear my own cries, like some wounded animal.

You can cry for a long time, but not forever. On the bureau facing me was a shot Daisy had taken of me and Edgardo at the beach, drinking the same piña colada out of two straws, and another of the two of us with Eddie when he was a baby. I got up, grabbed the beach picture and threw it against the wall. The tinkle of falling glass didn't make me feel any better.

I lay down again. By this time the fury I had felt at the lawyer's was gone. All that was left was an empty pit in my stomach and a fuzzy feeling in my head. If I divorced Edgardo, would I have enough money for Eddie to go for a Master's degree in the States? Should I go back to New York or stay in Puerto Rico? Thoughts whirled around, but I couldn't get hold of them. My brain was like an old car battery that jumpstarted and then sputtered out.

I didn't move when I heard the key in the door. Edgardo called out my name, but I didn't answer. I was lying on the bed with my face to the wall when he entered the room. He lay down next to me, his body encircling mine, reminding me that what I thought belonged to me wasn't mine anymore.

We both lay there in silence for a long time. Edgardo finally arose, picked up the picture of the two of us at the beach, put it back on the bureau, and left the room. I closed my eyes, and didn't open them until I heard him sweeping up the glass.

He gave me a hand to get up from the bed. I hadn't noticed it before, but my neck hurt as he pulled me up. I let him guide me to the living room and sit me down on the sofa.

"We have to talk," he said, taking a chair opposite me.

"Yeah."

"Maggie, please forgive me. I love you and Eddie. I don't want to lose you."

I said nothing.

"I lost my way. Please help me get back on the right track."

"It's over, Edgardo."

"Maggie, please."

I kept quiet.

"You want me to move out?"

I shrugged. Our family was broken. What did the details matter?

"Look Maggie, please don't abandon me now. I promise you I'll be a new man. Don't kick me when I'm down. Just stand by me until this is over. Then, if you still want a divorce, I won't stand in your way."

Forget about becoming a new man. I wanted the old Edgardo back, the man who had never heard of thousand dollar dinners. The man who thought me and Eddie were more important than anything else in the whole world.

"I'll sleep in the guest room," he said softly.

I wondered whether this was what the lawyer had told him to say, advising him that it was important to be sure the wife is on board and ready to stand by her man, just in case it hits the newspapers, or goes to court. "You've got to humor her," Álvarez would have said.

My old Edgardo would never have thought of separate bedrooms. For years we couldn't get enough of each other. Whenever I went for a few days to New York, he complained it was hard to fall asleep without me beside him.

I looked at him.

"I mean, of course, if that's you want," he added softly, smiling at me, uncertainty in his eyes.

What I wanted was to wipe the sticky smile off his face.

"I crashed the BMW."

"What?"

"I hit an SUV."

"The Beamer, is it bad?" Edgardo's voice rose in spite of his efforts to keep it under control.

"Maybe you should take a look." I held out the keys.

He took them and went out the door.

After a few minutes he came back and yelled, "Jesus Christ, Maggie, you totaled my car."

"I'm sure it can be fixed. The insurance will cover it."

"No, it's a total loss, believe me. You have no idea how I loved that car." He sat down and cradled his head in his hands.

"Whatever the insurance won't cover, you can take out of the divorce settlement," I told him.

Edgardo didn't answer. He just sat there staring at the ground.

"You never asked me whether I'm hurt," I said.

Edgardo lifted his head to stare at me. "Maggie, I'm so sorry. I'm not thinking straight. You look fine."

"Appearances can be deceiving."

"Sweetheart, tell me, are you okay?"

I massaged my neck with my hand. "Not really." I said, blinking back the tears. Starting to cry again would mean collapsing into a heap of howling pain.

"What's wrong with your neck?' asked Edgardo. "Whiplash?"

Still fighting back tears, I forced myself to move my head from side to side, slowly and gingerly. "I don't think it's that bad."

"I'll take you to the doctor."

"Going to the doctor isn't going to help."

The Pinch of the Crab

"Maggie, are you sure you're okay?"
I shook my head.
"For God's sake, tell me what's wrong."
"Internal injuries."
He looked at me.
I stared back.
Edgardo's smile died before it was born.

Fallen Branches

The backyard is half covered by fallen branches of the mango tree, glossy green leaves turning brown. Katia steps gingerly over a broken glass louver and sits down on the thickest branch of the giant tree, about two feet in diameter. The ridges of the rough bark make her fingers tingle. Eyes clenched tight, she digs her nails into the pulpy furrows. What if all the branches were to rise and rejoin the pitiful stump? Her flower garden, smothered under the debris of Hurricane Maria would miraculously reappear.

A cool breeze rumples her hair, bringing a sudden whiff of the odor of death. What's that rustling? Ginger, the Golden Retriever, searching in the dead leaves, body tense with expectation. Katia shudders, and whistles to the dog. She worked hard with her husband Pablo to locate all the carp after the little fish pond was destroyed by crashing branches of the mango tree. Ugh! A dead fish must be hiding somewhere slowly rotting.

It's early in the morning, but the clouds are clearing and the breeze is dying away. The intense heat of the sun prickles her face and arms. Moisture rises from the wet earth like steam from a sauna. She hastens into the house and puts a pot on the gas burner to heat up water for coffee.

Pablo enters the kitchen and reaches for a napkin to wipe his forehead. "I couldn't sleep. It's hot as hell."

"Yeah. A mosquito was singing in my ear all night."

What to eat? A cereal box is on the counter, but the milk has gone bad. Surprising it stayed fresh for so long with no electricity. Katia pulls out a box of pancake mix, thinking of using the gas burner, but then puts it back. You can't make decent pancakes without milk. Better to keep it simple, just serve sliced bread with butter and jam. Anyway, nothing will taste good with that dead fish smell seeping into the house.

She nibbles her bread while watching Pablo eat, his square jaw moving up and down, bearing down on large bites. He finishes off three slices, munching with good appetite. "I've got a half tank of gas. Let's go see what happened to the apartment."

Katia doesn't want to go. The apartment, where they lived before their son was born, is probably a wreck. But hey, staying all day in the house, doesn't seem like a great option either. Who wants to sit in a living room with windows replaced by plywood sheets that block the light? Her shoulder twitches. She reaches up and presses her ears with her forefingers for a few seconds. Stop thinking about roaring winds ripping through the house. Picking up shards of glass mixed with leaves from the floor afterwards, and then ringing out mops over and over to get rid of half a foot of water, wasn't too much fun either.

Who knows when they will be able to install new windows. Pablo had a hard time contacting Jorge, the Dominican handyman. The poor guy had stayed with his wife and son in his pickup truck for two days, because his house was flooded and there were no roads open. He came by and took measurements, but it turned out that there were no replacements available for the glass louvers. Suppliers were either sold out or had closed shop.

Katia gets up to place the remains of her bread in the trash. "Are you sure we should drive? There are no traffic lights. Maybe we should wait a couple of days before going to the apartment."

"Wait for what? The Governor is talking about restoring electricity by Christmas. Over two months from now. We've already waited too long to check on the apartment. Let's go in your car. It's older."

Yeah, sure. What does it matter to him if her car gets crashed, and she is left without transportation? But maybe Pablo has a point. His Audi is only a couple of years old, and her twelve-year-old Toyota is worth almost nothing. Since the hurricane struck, they've been acting like a couple again. Not that they are lovey-dovey or anything, but emergencies call for cooperation.

The hurricane even made a friend of Myrna, the widow next door who griped for years about a branch of the mango tree invading her yard, filling it up with refuse, falling leaves and rotting fruits. When Katia pointed out that the mangos were delicious, Myrna retorted that she didn't like mangos, too damn sweet and spongy. Just imagine, a native-born Boricua who hates mangos! But now that the offensive branch is down, Myrna has become very sweet. She even brought over two gallons of bottled water when the water drained out of Katia's cistern. Years of feuding gone with the wind!

Although it's Katia's car, Pablo insists on driving. When they enter the parking lot of the apartment building, she sees lots of windows boarded up. Not a good sign. The guard in the lobby tells them the elevators aren't working.

"But the building has a generator to power the common areas."

"Yeah, but the elevators were flooded."

Katia grips the railing tightly as she follows Pablo up the stairwell, her eyes slowly adjusting to the dim lights. They climb the last two flights groping the walls in complete darkness to reach the twelfth floor. Pablo struggles with the key to the apartment door. Why did she agree to come? It's going to be a total disaster, water and broken glass everywhere. One last twist and the door is open. The windows held. Everything's okay, except for a stagnant pool of water in the living room, which must have seeped under the sliding glass doors that open to a small balcony. Nothing that can't be fixed with a mop and pail.

After wringing out the mop, Katia joins Pablo on the balcony. "Lucky we put in storm windows."

The Pinch of the Crab

"Yeah. But look, the paint on the balcony wall is all bubbled up. I'll have to bring a scraper and a roller next time."

"Minor compared to what could have happened." Katia wipes her wet hands on her jeans. "You can move back in once the elevators are working."

Pablo presses a paint bubble with his finger and water oozes out. "There's no electricity and no water." He peels off a couple of strips of ruined paint. "And you need help getting the house back in shape, don't you?"

"Yes, of course."

Pablo is quiet on the drive back. As he parks the car in the driveway, Katia remarks that driving without traffic lights wasn't so bad. People were amazingly considerate, signaling them to go first with a wave of the hand, or by turning their front lights on and off.

Pablo shrugs. "We'll see how long *that* lasts."

He's right. Civility on the road might be only temporary, a short-term expression of solidarity after the hurricane. Pablo is refusing to look at her, standing off to the side while she fumbles in her purse for the key. The sky has turned dark, and a light rain is falling. He takes his own key from his pocket, approaches the door, and then turns to look back at her.

"Katia, you..."

"What is it?"

"You didn't wait very long to remind me I don't belong here."

"I didn't mean it that way."

But she did mean it that way. One hundred per cent. She had been separated from Pablo for half a year when Maria struck. For several months before the separation, he had become very secretive, checking his cellphone constantly, guarding it from her, turning the dial face away so she couldn't see. When the damn phone rang, he would glance at it and not answer, not important he would say, and then twenty minutes later, he would disappear, giving some excuse about filling up his car, or buying new razors from the pharmacy, whatever. Then her old car broke down and it turned out that there was not nearly as much money in his account as there should have been, and they couldn't buy a new one. She had to get the creaky old

Toyota repaired. Katia put two and two together. He tried to persuade her that it was a mid-life crisis. "Lots of men go through it," he told her. "Even some women." She asked him to move out. Now he is back again.

Pablo opens the front door and gestures for her to enter the house first. Katia reaches for the light switch in the living room to dispel the gloom, but, of course, the light doesn't go on, because they haven't been able to find diesel for the generator.

Pablo is right behind her. "Katia, we need to talk."

"First things first. We need to eat something."

It's thundering now, and the partially boarded up kitchen is so dark she can hardly see. She calls out to Pablo to bring a lantern.

Katia doesn't feel up to a serious talk. She has to think things through. Their relationship involves more than just the two of them. She had thought she didn't have to worry about the separation upsetting their son, because he was already grown up. And not just an adult, a successful one. Gabriel finished his Master's in Business Administration at the University of Puerto Rico, landed a job in telecommunications, married and bought a house in the suburbs of San Juan. But she was completely wrong about Gaby's reaction to his parent's separation. He was upset. Terribly upset. He and his wife Jessica couldn't talk about anything else. A marriage that lasted thirty-five years shouldn't be broken lightly. You and Papi should get counseling.

Pablo was adamant about not opening up about the causes of the breach. But it wasn't easy for Katia to hold back, especially when Gaby kept talking about not letting the little stuff spoil a great relationship. If only he knew half the real story.

Once it was announced that Hurricane Maria could hit as a category five, Gaby had called her: "Papi shouldn't stay in that apartment on the twelfth floor. Higher floors are more vulnerable. And Mami, you'll need a man in the house. You two will be safer together."

Gaby was right. The hurricane was terrifying even with a companion. When the glass louvers in the living room blew out, Katia panicked. It was

The Pinch of the Crab

Pablo who had enough presence of mind to grab her hand and rush into the master bedroom. Together they pushed the chest of drawers in front of the door, and watched it shake for several hours, huddled on the bed. They have been together ever since, working as a team to get things back in shape. So, maybe she should say something to take the sting out of her remark about Pablo returning to the apartment.

Pablo enters the kitchen with a lantern. She hands him a match. It lights up, sputters and goes out.

"Damn it." He tries again, this time with success.

"Good job." Katia smiles at him. "You know, I didn't mean to rush you. You're welcome to stay here as long as needed."

Pablo sighs. "I thought we should rethink things. About our separation, I mean." His eyes search her face.

Katia really does not want to go there. Now that she's apologized, why does he have to keep pushing? The trip to the apartment was exhausting, and the immediate problem is what to do about lunch. There's hardly anything to eat in the house. The supermarkets are finally open, but only accepting cash, the ATM machines aren't working, and the banks are closed. Between the two of them, they have only a hundred dollars. Forget about the future of the marriage. Getting through the next week is the real problem.

She goes to the cupboard, grabs a loaf of bread, and starts making a couple of sandwiches with canned tuna fish. It takes forever to open the goddamn can, because the expensive electric can opener Pablo gave her for Christmas several years ago is useless, and the old-fashioned one is rusty. Before mixing in some mayonnaise, she takes the jar closer to the lantern to get enough light to be sure there isn't any mold.

Pablo doesn't lift a finger to help make lunch. He is as conservative about gender roles as her grandfather—may he rest in peace.

She places the sandwiches and bottled water on the dining room table and calls Pablo.

"Not your best," he says after a few bites.

"What?"

Pablo attempts to smile. "Don't get mad. I know you don't have all the ingredients."

"Don't eat if you don't like it." Katia suppresses the urge to grab the half sandwich left on his plate and fling it at the wall. She gets up, leaving her own sandwich untouched.

"What's wrong? Aren't you hungry?"

"No, too tired. I'll go and lie down for a while."

She stretches out on the bed, her stomach growling. It's still raining. Damn Pablo, she *is* hungry. Even worse than hunger, is the rising rage in her gut. She wants him out of the house.

It was okay living with Pablo during the storm. After all they had thirty-five years together and a wonderful son. But how long is this emergency going to last? It's already mid-October, about a month has gone by since the hurricane, and only ten per cent of dwellings have electricity, mostly in tourist areas. Ordinary folks will be lucky if the lights come back on before Easter.

Her best friend, Ana Lucía, thinks Katia should see the hurricane as an opportunity to rethink divorcing Pablo. A few days ago, she called Katia and urged her to give the guy another chance. Oye, chica, piénsalo, it's no fun facing old age alone.

Katia shakes her head. Ana Lucía has got it all wrong. After the separation, Katia never felt lonely. Not once. What a relief it had been to be able to work long hours at her job as a lawyer without worrying about Pablo grumbling. During the marriage she put on a show of being a creative cook, but she found out that it was great to make a sandwich or eat leftovers. Even more important, she no longer had to think about Pablo's betrayals, no longer wondered whether something lacking in her made him turn to other women.

Of course, since Hurricane Maria they have been living together once again. Neither of them is working yet, so it's even more intense than before. You'd think the construction firm Pablo works for would have plenty of jobs to rebuild, but he hasn't been called in yet, because his boss is still

The Pinch of the Crab

struggling to replace equipment lost in the storm. Katia's boss at the law firm called to say the broken windows at the office had been replaced, and they had finally found a new electric generator. His hope was to get things going in two weeks. He explained that the firm had a severe cash flow crisis. She could pick up a check for half her salary. Once the firm got back on its feet, her full salary would be restored, but her time not working because of the hurricane would be counted as vacation.

Meanwhile, Katia is stuck with Pablo 24/7.

He's standing in the bedroom doorway. "Are you sleeping?"

"No, just resting."

"Katia, we really need to talk."

He comes in and sits on the bed, reaches for her hand, and holds it tight for a long moment. He loves her deeply, can't bear to lose her. He is terribly sorry about the girlie mess he got into, but he is a changed man.

"I mean that was just a passing thing. It didn't affect my love for you. You've forgiven me before. Can't you forgive me now?"

"What are you talking about?"

Pablo looks confused, stumbles over his words. Sorry to remind her, he is talking about Graciela.

He pronounces the name in an almost whisper, but it still has a sweet cadence. Graciela, the first of Pablo's extramarital affairs, a young woman Pablo knew in college and reconnected with at a conference. He told Katia that Graciela was her type of person, intelligent and well-informed. Let's invite her and her boyfriend over for dinner. Katia liked the way Graciela avoided small talk. They discussed whether the novel Isabel Allende's latest novel *Eva Luna* was as good as *The House of Spirits,* and whether the women characters were fully developed.

She had been blind. It took a while to catch on. Gaby was born several months after Graciela entered their lives, about the time the boyfriend disappeared. Gaby was a colicky baby, and there were many sleepless nights that first year. The baby absorbed Katia's attention and Pablo complained about being abandoned. That was his excuse. It was a rough patch, but Pablo finally decided to give up Graciela to save the marriage. She forgave Pablo.

It had been the right thing to do, but why was she feeling tightness in her throat at the mention of Graciela's name after so many years? And now he is telling her to forgive him again.

Katia pulls herself up to a sitting position on the bed, her face level with Pablo's.

"Please try to understand. It's not a question of forgiveness. I'm tired of living with suspicions. I don't want to go back to all that."

"Darling, please. We've been through so much together. Even a category five can't stop us. We're a team."

The lump in her throat eases. Should she give him another chance?

"Katia, my own darling, please say yes."

She hesitates, tears welling up from nowhere.

Pablo seizes her hand and looks into her eyes with what he must imagine is romantic fervor. "Sweetheart, believe me, that girl didn't mean anything to me."

Katia moves sideways to put more space between them. "What did you say?"

In a low voice, Pablo repeats that the girl really didn't mean anything.

Yeah, sure. He had been infatuated with a nineteen-year-old idiot. She could still see Pablo's mooning face gazing expectantly at his cell phone. Paloma was her name. Not exactly a symbol of peace.

"How dare you tell me she didn't mean anything? You emptied our bank account for a girl who meant nothing? What does that say about you?"

"It was a terrible mistake."

His words bring back the whole sordid story. Pablo met Paloma in a barber shop where she clipped his hair. She had never finished high school. Her ambition was to be a stylist in an upscale beauty salon. Supposedly she would be hired because of a special talent for doing nails in the latest glitter styles. Meanwhile she had found someone's husband to pay her bills. Katia suffered when Pablo fell in love with Graciela, but at least she was

The Pinch of the Crab

intelligent and charming, someone you could imagine a man of substance falling for.

"A mistake? What do you mean, Pablo? Don't tell me you didn't know what you were doing. You cheated on me and robbed me for some worthless puta. And now you expect me to go back to you?"

"Please Katia, understand. I wasn't myself."

"That's where we disagree." Katia stands up. "You were yourself. YOU SHOWED ME EXACTLY WHO YOU REALLY ARE. Pablo el idiota, Pablo el pendejo, PABLO THE SHMUCK."

Pablo also stands up, his face flushed. "Is this what you really think of me?"

Ginger comes over to Katia and noses her hand. Katia bends down for a moment to rub the fur on the back of the dog's neck, trying to calm herself, but that hard rim of anger, that desire to tell Pablo to get the hell out of her life, is back again.

"Yes, that's exactly what I think of you and I want you to leave."

"To hell with everything, then, after all I've done to help you put the house back together, you're treating me like scum. It wasn't that way when I saved you, pulled you into the bedroom when the wind broke the windows. You were grateful then, weren't you? Held me tight."

Pablo pushes her back onto the bed and holds her down by the arms. "You wanted me to make love to you, didn't you? Answer me."

"Yes."

"And you enjoyed it, didn't you? Don't lie to me."

Katia nods. He is holding her arms down so hard it hurts. She has no choice but to admit wanting it, enjoying it, even if it isn't true, but it *is* true. No use explaining to Pablo that things like that can happen, especially in the middle of a hurricane. He of all people should understand that passionate sex doesn't always mean until death do us part.

"You're an ungrateful bitch. Why couldn't I see it for all those years? You don't deserve a man like me." Pablo releases his hold on her, and moves away from the bed. "I'm leaving and taking Ginger with me."

Fallen Branches

At the mention of her name, Ginger looks up at Pablo. Her tail wags for a moment and then becomes still.

Katia sits up, her feet shuffling on the floor, searching for her flip-flops. "Don't be silly. Ginger will be miserable in the apartment. We agreed she would stay with me until you find a bigger place. And the elevator's not working."

"Oh, so you're worried about Ginger, but you don't give a damn if I have to walk up twelve flights, do you?"

Katia rubs the red spot on her arm where he held her down. "You're always complaining about the gym closing down after the hurricane, aren't you?"

Pablo comes closer. "WHAT? Say that again?"

She has gone too far. Suggesting that climbing the stairs would be good exercise was downright mean. Of course, calling her a bitch because she didn't want to renew their vows wasn't nice either, but best to avoid further confrontation. She tells Pablo he is welcome to stay until the elevators get fixed.

Pablo shrugs, and settles himself into the armchair near the chest of drawers, his stocky frame solid and immobile.

Katia leans back on her pillow, and closes her eyes. Pablo says nothing. When she opens them, he is still sitting there. She gets up and tells him their talk isn't finished yet. She wants to make one thing crystal clear. This is a temporary arrangement until the elevators get fixed. "You know, if it wasn't for the hurricane, we would already be divorced."

"Shut the hell up. I wish we were divorced. I don't want to be married to a fucking bitch like you one more minute. Get the hell out of the bedroom so I can pack my stuff."

"Okay." Katia starts toward the door.

He grabs her by the shoulder. "Not so fast."

"You're hurting me."

Pablo tightens his grip, holds on for a long moment, and then jerks her before letting go. Katia teeters for a moment before regaining her

The Pinch of the Crab

balance. Suppressing the urge to run, she walks out of the bedroom into the kitchen and puts the remains of her lunch in the garbage, her hands shaking. Thuds and shuffling sounds from the direction of the bedroom are followed by rapid footsteps.

Pablo pokes his head in to say he will leave Ginger with her for now. He's carrying the large blue suitcase purchased years ago for their Caribbean cruise. "I'll come back for the gun later."

Katia wants to tell him to take the goddamn gun, she doesn't want it in the house, but she keeps quiet. He marches out, slamming the front door so hard that the house shakes.

Katia walks into the bedroom and checks the safe. It's securely locked. Good. When Pablo bought the gun, he urged her to learn how to shoot, but she wanted nothing to do with guns. Then or now. After all, aren't more kids killed in accidents involving their fathers' guns than by burglars?

Gaby must have been about two years old when a crime wave spurred Pablo to apply for a gun permit. He wanted to keep it in the drawer of the bedside table, so he would have easy access in case of a break-in. No way was Katia going to let him leave a loaded gun where a toddler could find it. Pablo ranted on and on about how a man is not a man unless he can protect his family. Besides, as a United States citizen he had a constitutional right to own a gun. She threatened to move out and take Gaby with her. He finally locked the gun in a safe in their bedroom closet, where it stayed except for target practice.

Now that Pablo is gone the house is quiet. The rain has stopped. Katia keeps busy cleaning for half an hour and then gets into her car to check on the nearest ATM machine. There's a line, a good sign, because the machine is working. She takes out a couple of hundred and returns home. The sun has just set and shadows invade the house. She checks the kitchen drawer to be sure the flashlight is there, testing it to be sure it works before lighting a couple of lanterns.

A loud knocking at the door startles her. Is Pablo back? What will she say to him? But it's the neighbor, Myrna, the widow who hates mangos and gave her bottled water. Someone just told her diesel was available at a Total Gas Station not too far away.

"Tell Pablo about it," Myrna says.

"He's gone back to the apartment."

"Oh." Myrna looks like she is about to ask what's going on, but thinks better of it. "Why don't *you* come with me, Katia? Let's try our luck, get up early before the line gets too long."

The next day they go and wait on a line of cars for three hours. Katia returns triumphant with several buckets of diesel. Just as she is trying to figure out how to get the diesel from the buckets into the generator, a diesel truck stops and honks. Her house is first on his list of deliveries now that new supplies have become available. Wow! She will have light in the evening. Things get even better the next day. The handyman calls to say he will come by to take care of the fallen mango tree, and her boss calls to tell her the law firm will open the following week.

No word from Pablo, but maybe that's just as well. Then Gaby calls and asks his mother how she's doing, but once Katia says everything is okay, his tone changes. How could she throw his father out of the house knowing full well that the elevators aren't working at the apartment? She tries to explain that it's not so simple. Gaby tells her he's in Santurce for a business meeting. Can he come over later in the afternoon to talk this over?

"Of course." Katia puts her phone down slowly.

She forgot to ask what time he would be coming. But she shouldn't call back. He might be in an important meeting. Her dear Gaby, always steady and responsible. While her friends struggled with children who got into all sorts of trouble, she had never worried about her son.

When Gaby arrives, she rushes into the kitchen to get coffee and cookies, but all he wants is water. He perches on the sofa, leaning forward, his back hunched over.

The way Gaby's knee is jiggling reminds her of an incident many years ago, when he got very angry with his father. Gaby wanted to go on an excursion organized by his school that meant taking a small boat to

The Pinch of the Crab

Mona Island, a trip Pablo thought was too dangerous. The channel between Mona Island and Puerto Rico is very deep and subject to sudden storms. Gaby yelled that the school would never make dangerous travel arrangements, and he deserved to go because his grades were excellent. Katia remembers the word he used. His father was being unjust.

Now Gaby lifts his head and looks at Katia as though she were a stranger. He can't believe that she made his father move back to the apartment. "Mami, whatever got into you? This is not like you. It's so unfair. How can you be so cruel?"

He has lots more to say. Since the hurricane, whole communities in Puerto Rico are pulling together. The papers are filled with stories about generous acts to help the less fortunate, neighbors who risked their lives to get people in wheelchairs to safety before the flood waters rose. Meanwhile, his mother threw his father out like trash.

His words feel like a hard blow to the stomach with a blunt instrument. For a moment Katia just sits there thinking he is right. She has been cruel and selfish. But then the fire of indignation rises in her gut. Pablo did not tell their son the whole truth, but only a small part of the story that would turn Gaby against her. She protected Pablo, never even hinting that infidelity was the cause of the separation. Now he no longer deserves her silence.

The words come tumbling out. She tells Gaby everything, all about his father's affairs and how he gave money to the latest puta, money that was not his alone, money that belonged to the family. And it was a lie to say she threw him out. It was Pablo's decision to leave because she wouldn't agree to give the marriage another chance.

It feels good telling the truth, letting all her anguish out. Gaby lets her finish without interruption.

"Mami, I wish you didn't tell me this."

"I'm sorry. I just couldn't bear for you to think I'm the one responsible for the divorce."

Gaby is silent for a long moment. Then he shakes his head, as though trying to get rid of the ugliness in the air. "Look Mami, I'm glad you told me, and I understand how you feel. But try to understand how Papi feels. He kept telling me how the two of you braved the hurricane together, and he was so sure that whatever had gone wrong with the marriage was all right again. And he was terribly hurt that you don't want him to stay. Mami, I know he behaved badly. I also know Papi really loves you, deeply loves you."

So typical of her son. Telling her to try to see it standing in the other guy's shoes.

"Gaby, I understand that Papi is hurt. But after all that's happened, I can't live with him. I don't want him in the same house. It's not a feeling that I can reason away."

To tell the truth, Pablo's presence had become so irksome she didn't want him to touch her, but that was something she couldn't share with Gaby. Why has she been feeling physical repulsion so soon after making love to him in the midst of the hurricane? It doesn't make sense even to her.

Mother and son talk it over. He appeals to her most vulnerable side, telling her that he knows her inner being, believes she is truly a forgiving person. "Don't make a final decision now, Mami," he says before leaving.

Two weeks pass by. No word from father or son. Then Gaby calls and talks about going fishing with his father. By some miracle, his best friend's boat survived the hurricane although most of the other boats in the marina were badly damaged.

"How is Papi doing?" Katia asks.

"He's depressed."

"I'm sorry. I was thinking of calling him, but I'm not sure he would like to hear from me."

"I've never seen him like this. That's why I'm taking him fishing. Get his mind off things."

"You're doing the right thing."

"Mami, you haven't changed your mind, have you?"

"No, please understand. I can't."

The Pinch of the Crab

After a short pause, Gaby says he understands. "Oh, I forgot to mention Papi wants to take Ginger along."

"Fine, she'll love it."

"I'll come by early tomorrow morning, and pick her up."

Should she worry about this conversation? Before the hurricane, Pablo accepted the divorce. He wasn't cheerful about it, but he wasn't super depressed. Why is he falling apart now?

Maybe some coffee with crackers and cheese will make her feel better. She puts her cell phone down, goes into the kitchen, and opens the fridge. The chunk of Gouda is full of mold. Food spoils quickly when you only keep the generator on for twelve hours a day. She throws the cheese toward the trash can, and it falls to the floor with a thud. Is Pablo sad depressed or angry depressed? In their thirty-five years of marriage, he never hit her. She hasn't told Gaby about Pablo pushing her down on the bed or grabbing her shoulder, but there is no reason to. Once she told Pablo he was hurting her, he stopped, let her go. Stop worrying, just pick up the goddamn cheese, and put it in the garbage. Going on a boat trip with his son is the best medicine for Pablo.

Her friend Ana Lucía calls and suggests a shopping trip to Plaza las Americas mall to help them recover from the hurricane blues. The lights are finally on, she says. Katia doesn't want to buy anything, but she goes anyway. Ana Lucía is right about it being therapeutic. As Katia walks down the wide air-conditioned aisles between the gleaming lights of high-end stores she forgets about the roofless houses, the trees with bare branches, and the electric cables dangling uselessly from leaning poles that look like they are about to topple. She hurries past the sports store where she bought a present for Pablo a couple of years before.

Saturday is fine, because of the mall expedition, but on Sunday Katia has nothing planned. She tries to keep busy, cleaning the bathrooms with a product that claims to be effective in preventing mold. Her eyes smart. She must have breathed in too much of the chemicals.

She lies down on the bed and opens the windows, hoping fresh air will make the nausea go away, but there's no breeze, and no Ginger to come and nuzzle her.

Katia makes an effort to burp, and belches up something warm and foul-tasting. If only she hadn't told Gaby about his father's infidelity. She should have had the strength to take the blame for the divorce on herself. She throws up in the toilet, and then rinses her mouth over and over until the foul taste disappears. Exhausted, she lies down again.

She must have napped. When her cell phone sounds, the room is almost dark. Still only half awake, she grabs for the phone. It's Gaby. He's back from the fishing expedition, but he won't be able to deliver Ginger. As soon as he got back on shore, he noticed multiple calls from his wife Jessica. Their little girl Isabela had thrown up several times, and she couldn't reach the pediatrician.

"Oh my God, is Isabelita all right?"

"Yeah, she's feeling much better. Jessica was about to take her to Emergency, but I persuaded her to wait. Isabelita hasn't thrown up again. She's drinking Gatorade right now."

"Thank goodness."

"Papi said he would drop off Ginger."

"Okay. How was the trip?"

"Pretty good, but I'm still worried about Papi." Gaby describes how his father put on an act of being into fishing, but his mind was elsewhere. And the strange thing is that even going back to work at the construction firm hasn't helped. "Papi worked for a few days, and then called in sick."

"That's odd. He's always loved his job."

Gaby thinks his father is falling into a clinical depression. "You know the suicide rate has gone up since the hurricane."

"Gaby, you're not serious, are you?"

No, Gaby didn't mean to alarm his mother, but he does think his father should see a psychologist to help him get through the separation. The problem is how to persuade his father he needs help.

Katia can hear her little granddaughter crying in the background.

"We'll talk more tomorrow," says Gaby.

"Yeah. Isabela needs you now. Lots of love to her and Jessica."

After hanging up, Katia still feels groggy, so she steps onto the small balcony of the master bedroom overlooking the backyard. In the deepening twilight, a light breeze rumples the new leaves that have sprouted on the trunk of the fallen mango tree.

The doorbell rings. Startled, Katia quickly goes back inside. The doorbell rings again. Could Pablo be here already? No, it's too soon for him to make it from the dock. Must be the neighbor. Plantains disappeared from the supermarkets after the hurricane, but Myrna found some at a roadside stand, and promised to bring over some of the mofongo dish she was making. Katia stands in front of the door, listening, before opening it.

It's Pablo with Ginger. The dog jumps on Katia and licks her face affectionately. Pablo stands there, on the steps, not saying anything.

"How was the trip?"

Pablo shrugs. "Nothing is good anymore." His eyes are fixed on a flowering hibiscus next to the stoop. He reaches for a red petal and crushes it with his fingers.

"Can I come in?" He still isn't looking at her. "I need to get my gun."

Katia hesitates. Gaby is worried his father might be suicidal. Ginger pushes past her into the house. When she draws back to let the dog go by, Pablo steps forward. The moment to refuse him entry has passed.

"Of course," she says, gesturing for him to come in. "Would you like a coke, or some water?"

He shakes his head. "I just want the gun."

Katia sits down on the sofa in the living room while he goes to the safe in the closet of the bedroom. The second hand on the wall clock goes tick-ticking round and round. Why is he taking so long? She drums her fingers on the arm of the sofa and then sits still, listening, discerning faint footfalls becoming louder.

Pablo stands in the doorway. "You left the balcony door open. Not a good idea." He sits down heavily on the love seat opposite her, the gun cradled in his hand. "Come to think of it, I'm thirsty. I will have a coke."

When Katia gets up to get the drink, he tells her to forget it. "Sit down, we have to talk."

She sinks back down on the sofa.

"You broke your promise," he says, looking at her for the first time. He puts the gun on the coffee table, picks it up, stroking the butt with his thumb and forefinger, and puts it back down.

"What promise?"

"DON'T GIVE ME THAT SHIT," he yells. "You know damn well what fucking promise I'm talking about. When we decided to separate you made a solemn promise never to tell Gaby anything. Don't try to deny it."

True enough. The price of his agreement to the divorce was her promise to keep silent about his infidelities, never tell anyone, especially not their son. Katia stares at him. It never crossed her mind that her son would tell. Gaby must have been trying to explain to his father how hurt she was by the affair with a girl young enough to be her daughter.

Pablo demands an answer. "Come on, don't lie to me. You told him, didn't you?"

She freezes, unable to speak. He gets up and hits her hard across the face. She screams between sobs for him to stop.

"Shut the fuck up," he says, and then sits down again, pulling the gun toward him.

The blood trickling down from her nose tastes salty. Ginger comes bounding into the room, and rushes up to her mistress, whining softly. Katia pats her until she quiets down and lies at her feet.

"NOW YOU FUCKING BITCH, TELL ME THE TRUTH, DID YOU BREAK YOUR PROMISE NEVER TO TELL GABY?"

"Yes, but you told him that I had been cruel to you, kicked you out of the house. You made me out to be a monster. You told your side, so I had to tell my side. You didn't tell him what you put me through year after year, one puta after another. And now you call me a bitch and hit me, make me bleed? Who's the real monster? COME ON, PABLO, TELL ME, WHO IS THE REAL MONSTER?

Pablo shakes his head. "There you go again, twisting everything, but you can't get out of this one. You made a solemn promise and you broke it. You ruined my life."

"What have you done to my life?"

"SHUT UP. YOU DESPISE ME. AND NOW, BECAUSE OF YOU, MY SON DESPISES ME, TOO."

He picks up the gun and points it toward the wedding picture on the opposite wall.

"What a fool I was. You were so pretty and so sweet, and I didn't know the real you." He takes aim at the photo. Then he turns around and points the gun at the dog, busy licking her foot. "Do you love Ginger?"

"Pablo, what are you doing? Ginger is your dog as much as mine. You love her, too. Please, Pablo, you're not crazy, this isn't you, stop, please."

"That's right, I do love Ginger, but I want to kill her and then myself. Why not? Tell me, what's left for me? I loved you, too. You know that, don't you?"

Slowly Pablo moves the barrel of the gun to point toward Katia.

A little black hole dances in front of her eyes and then holds steady at the center of her universe. A clap of thunder sounds and the tiny spot of black starts to grow, flowing outward, looming larger and larger until all is darkness.

She doesn't hear the second shot.

Myrna was ladling half of the mofongo dish she had cooked into a porcelain bowl to take over to her neighbor's house when one quick staccato after another rang out. Must be those crazy teenagers across the street playing with firecrackers again, she told herself, and proceeded to carry the bowl to Katia's house. No one answered the bell. She opened the door with one hand, cradling the mofongo with the other.

"Katia?"

Crossing the foyer into the living room, Myrna gasped, and the bowl crashed to the floor. Her screams brought another neighbor who called 911. When the police arrived, there were two bodies lying in the living room. Blood was all over the floor, spotted with shards of porcelain and pieces of mashed plantain. They had to lock Ginger into a bedroom before examining the crime scene.

The obituary Gabriel published in the paper mourned the loss of both parents. It was a kind obituary, not casting blame, just mourning the terrible tragedy that took his loved ones away. Katia would have said it sounded just like her dear Gaby.

Heavy Downpour

A sudden gust of wind lifted the exam papers on the coffee table and scattered them at my feet. I rushed to the balcony that overlooked the Atlantic. In the tropical sunshine, the waves close to shore were bright turquoise fading into deep blue as the eye moved further out. Billowing gray clouds were piling up on the horizon, streaked with rain. After each dart of lightning, I counted the seconds to see how long it would take to hear the boom of thunder.

The runners of the sliding windows were corroded by the salt air. By the time I had closed them and sat back down to finish correcting exams, I was dripping with sweat, my thin blouse sticking to my skin. I went down the hallway to check on my five-year-old daughter who was fast asleep in the bedroom. The intercom buzzer rang. I rushed to answer before she woke up, thinking it could be the postman with the parcel my mother had sent special delivery for her birthday.

"Hola. ¿Quién es?"

"Soy yo. Michael."

I rang the buzzer to let him in. I hadn't seen Michael Pierce for about a year. I used to see him and Estella every month or so, but he had disappeared from those American parties in Puerto Rico, not that I could blame him. There was entirely too much drinking and constant whining about the heat,

The Pinch of the Crab

the traffic, and the general lack of efficiency. At one of these parties, Mike had proposed a toast, "To Puerto Rico! Love it or leave it!" An uneasy silence followed. When we got home my husband Jeff told me, "Of course, he's right, but it's hard to leave when Eli Lilly pays better here than in the States."

When I opened the door, I noticed Mike's curly hair was disheveled and wet, but that wasn't surprising because the storm had moved in to shore, and the rain was pounding on the balcony windows. He wore shorts, long socks and beaten-up tennis shoes. I ushered him into the living room.

"What a beautiful view," he said, running his fingers through his hair and gazing through the balcony window facing the ocean. I followed his eyes and saw that the approaching storm had kicked up furious whitecaps.

"Sit down," I told him.

"I'm kind of sweaty from running," he said.

"Don't worry about it. I'll get you something cool to drink."

I left him perched gingerly on the sofa, and went into the kitchen.

As I was getting the ice out from the fridge, I thought about Mike. His full name was Michael Pierce Ramírez, son of an American father and a Puerto Rican mother. I had first met him in college in the late sixties. He was very much involved in radical movements just as I had been in those days. He often spoke to meetings of the Students for a Democratic Society about imperialism in his native land of Puerto Rico.

I myself had become disillusioned with the SDS and had moved into a women's consciousness-raising group. I was going out with a very dominating political type who constantly berated me for being a timid WASP with middle class values. The feminist group helped me navigate my way out of *that* relationship. I found Michael more sympathetic than the guy I was going out with, but somehow nothing worked out romantically. We picked up our friendship again when I moved to the island in 1971.

I placed a pitcher of lemonade on the coffee table and poured two glasses. Mike drank thirstily and asked for more. He downed the second glass in several gulps, picked up some exam papers, and glanced through them.

"I see you're still teaching English."

"Yeah."

"Your students aren't doing too well." He held up an exam covered with red marks.

"It's tough for them when they get to the University," I replied. "English isn't taught well in the public schools."

"That's not the real problem," said Michael.

It didn't surprise me that Michael thought he knew more about the problem than I did although he had no teaching experience. He was that kind of guy, extraordinarily bright and well read, but opinionated as hell.

"Well, of course, English is not their native tongue," I said.

"Exactly," said Michael. "They see it as an imposition of the colonial power."

"I don't know. Most of my students want to learn English to get ahead in the world."

"That's what colonialism does. It undermines the worth of native language and culture."

I didn't reply. He had a point, but it was a job with flexible hours that meant I could spend quality time with my daughter. Besides, I enjoyed teaching and my students liked me.

"Beautiful apartment you've got here," Mike remarked. "Eli Lilly must be doing very well."

I ignored this.

"If what you're saying is that anyone teaching English is an agent of U.S. imperialism," I said, "why are you working for an English language newspaper?"

"I'm not working for the *San Juan Star* anymore."

Come to think of it, I had not noticed Mike's byline recently. I wondered what had happened.

"Estella left me," said Mike added.

"I'm sorry."

"She thought she was the wife of a future Pulitzer Prize winner. But she made a mistake."

The Pinch of the Crab

"Mike, that's not fair."

Mike shrugged.

Estella, a poet and an independentista, had never struck me as a woman looking to snare a man with prospects. She was petite with a ready smile and a great sense of humor.

"Estella was in love with you," I told him.

Mike frowned. "She wanted to have a baby."

"But you didn't?"

"It's not that I don't like kids. But it's crazy to want to bring another human being into this miserable fucking world."

Ten years ago, I might have agreed with him, but not since my daughter Karen was born. Her existence made up for whatever was wrong with the world. Besides, if Mike had really cared about Estella, he wouldn't be hiding behind leftwing clichés when the woman he loved wanted a baby. But it was no use trying to explain this to him.

"Why did you leave the *San Juan Star*?" I asked.

"I just couldn't hack it any more. They wouldn't let me work on an important story."

Mike paused and began to run his fingers along the embroidered Guatemalan designs of the throw cushions on the couch where he was seated.

"We don't have to talk about it if you don't want to," I said.

"I want to, but you never know who's listening."

I looked at him, but he had not changed expression.

"There's no one here but me and my daughter," I told him. "Jeff's in New Orleans."

Mike got up and in a business-like fashion removed the cushions from the couch, running his fingers around each one and then around the frame, before replacing them neatly.

"Mike, what are you doing?"

"It could be bugged."

"Don't be silly."

He walked over to a painting by Roberto Moya depicting a mother bending over her child on a tricycle and peered at it. For a moment, I thought he was thinking about the baby he could have had with Estella.

"Moya has a special way with children," I remarked.

"Sentimental bullshit," said Mike. "He's gone commercial."

Still staring at the painting, he ran his fingers lightly round the frame. Then he removed the picture and examined the back. I noticed his right hand was shaking when he tried to replace it on the hook on the wall.

"Watch out!" I yelled, just as the picture fell with a thud. Luckily it was an oil painting that had been framed without glass.

"Calm down," said Mike. "It didn't break."

"Mike, what's wrong with you?"

"Nothing."

"That's OK. Just leave it there. I'll hang it again later," I told him.

Mike propped up the picture against the wall and sat down on the sofa.

"Carrie, I have to be careful. You remember Alfredo Jiménez, the independentista lawyer who was murdered?"

"You mean the one that defended the Teamster boss, Luis Santander, from corruption charges?"

"Sí. He did a beautiful job proving his innocence," Mike replied.

I nodded. I had followed the drama of the trial in the newspapers. Jiménez had won the case by convincing the jury that the chief witness against the labor leader, the one that alleged he saw money changing hands, was an underworld figure himself who would testify to anything the government asked to get off drug charges.

"Alfredo's death is a great loss," Mike continued, shaking his head. "La pérdida de un gran patriota. Did you know he lived across the street?"

"Yes. I knew him to say hello. I couldn't believe it when he was killed. I saw the blood on the sidewalk for days."

"Yeah. They said it was a carjacking."

"The other theory was that Jiménez himself was involved in drug trafficking," I pointed out.

"It's a smear campaign." Mike raised his voice. "The dead can't defend themselves."

"I never believed a word of it," I replied. "He was such a nice man. Always smiled and asked after my daughter."

"He became too popular after winning the case," said Mike. "Jiménez was the only man that could have forged an effective alliance between labor and pro-independence forces. They had to cut him down."

"So, you wanted the *San Juan Star* to dig further?"

"Yes, but I'm telling you this in confidence."

"I won't tell anyone, except Jeff, of course."

"Not even Jeff," Mike barked.

"OK," I replied, thinking it was best to go along since he was becoming really agitated.

"I was getting close to the truth. That's why they fired me."

"What are you doing now?"

"I launched my own investigation a year ago. I'm close to a major breakthrough," Mike said loudly, clenching his fist. "Someday justice will be done."

He brought his fist down hard on the coffee table. I reached out with one hand to steady his teetering lemonade glass.

Mike took my hand in his and looked into my eyes. "Carrie, there are dark forces blocking the light of truth."

Although the rainstorm had brought cooling breezes that took the edge off the glaring heat, he was sweating profusely. Mike had always been a man intensely absorbed in whatever interested him in the moment, it was part of his charm, but I had never seen him quite like this. I withdrew my hand. He continued talking.

"They're following me, but I'm not afraid. They will never be able to get me. I guess they won't be looking for me at the luxury Condado apartment of Eli Lilly's Vice President for Operations in Puerto Rico," he said with a smile.

"Mike, *who* do you think is following you?"

Heavy Downpour

"Don't worry, Carrie. I lost them just before coming here. I would never do anything to put you in danger."

"Do you want some more lemonade?" I asked, reaching for the pitcher. Michael didn't answer. I spilled some on the table while pouring.

"I'll get a sponge from the kitchen," I said, rising from my chair.

"NO, don't go. Carrie, look at me."

He was watching me intently.

"What is it?" I asked, sitting down again.

A streak of lightning was followed by a quick boom of thunder, loud and close. In the silence that followed came the question, "You weren't going to make a phone call, were you, to tell them I'm here?"

"Mike, don't talk nonsense. I'm your friend. And I don't even know who *they* are."

"I carry this." Mike drew out a knife that had been concealed in his thick running sock. "Just in case."

I sat very still, my eyes fixed on the pitcher, but I could see the knife in his hand.

"I'm a non-violent man," continued Mike, "but I'm not stupid. The CIA caught Alfredo unarmed, but not me."

The knife had a short handle but the blade was long and sharp.

"I can defend myself. Like this." Michael lunged, his knife tracing an arc through the air.

I heard a wail from the back bedroom. My little girl must have been awakened by the thunder. I froze. The cries rose and fell, like the crescendos of a symphony. "Mommy, MOMMY, mommy, MOMMYYYYY!"

Michael laid the knife in front of him on the table. "What's wrong?" he asked. "Sounds like a baby crying."

"That's my daughter. She'll be five the day after tomorrow."

"Why don't you pick it up?" he asked, looking puzzled, as though he didn't remember Karen, or the lovely hand-crocheted baby dress with matching booties he and Estella had given me when she was born.

The Pinch of the Crab

"My daughter has a fever," I told him. "Now that she's awake I've got to take her to the doctor. We have to leave now." My fingers gripped the wooden arms of the chair to stop the shaking of my hands.

"I can take a hint," said Mike. "Far be it from me to make you neglect your motherly duties."

He smiled at me, slipped the knife back in his thick sock and got up.

I rose from my chair. "It's been so nice seeing you again," I said, giving him a peck on the cheek. "Take care of yourself."

"Don't worry, I will." He glanced down at his bulging sock.

I said goodbye and let him out. My daughter was still screaming, but I waited until I heard the elevator open and close. Then I latched and bolted the door.

I had to sit down for a moment on the chair in the foyer until my knees stopped shaking before running down the hallway to my daughter's room. I lifted her into my arms, cuddling her head against my shoulder. She quieted immediately. Her body was warm. For a moment I thought the lie I told Mike about Karen having a fever had become a self-fulfilling prophecy, but then I realized that it was just the normal warmth of a child waking from her nap. I could smell the sweet sweat on her hair. Still holding her tight, I reached over and bent one of the bedroom blinds down with my finger to look out the window that faced the street.

Water from the heavy downpour was still rushing along the gutters. Mike emerged from under the canopy that shaded the entrance to my building onto the sidewalk. He stopped at the curb, and looked to the right and the left before crossing the street to the other side. I watched him walk toward the traffic light at the corner, with that loping gait I knew so well. He still looked like a college kid with shorts, old tennis shoes and a tangled mop of curly hair. Just as I was about to let the blinds close, a well-dressed man in a suit crossed over to the same side of the street and walked in the same direction, about ten paces behind Mike. They both disappeared round the corner. I shuddered and held my daughter close.

DNA Blues

My iPhone beeped.

"Starbucks?"

Bianca Martínez was obviously cautious, texting me to meet in a public place, not the type to let a guy get some on the first date. But what the hell, the picture she had posted was *really* hot.

Although new to Puerto Rico, I was familiar with the Starbucks on Ashford Avenue, midway down the Condado tourist strip. I arrived on time for our coffee date. Better to let the girl make a late entrance. After ten minutes, I got nervous Bianca wouldn't show, and then there she was, standing awkwardly in the entrance, her eyes flitting from table to table.

She looked even better than her picture, slender, medium height with brown eyes, olive skin and soft dark curly hair. Not one of those girls who put up some doctored photo. Her hesitation at the door pleased me, too. Obviously, she wasn't an old hand at the online dating game.

Once her eyes met mine, I went over, introduced myself and beckoned her to join me at a table for two, off in a corner, away from a group of six guffawing teenagers. We started out talking about where we'd gone to college, SUNY Binghamton in her case, and Columbia in mine.

The Pinch of the Crab

When I got up to order at the counter, Bianca took out a tissue and wiped away the crumbs on the table. Whoever sat there before us must have been a real slob. I brought back two coffee lattes, 'grande' for me and tall for her. She smiled at me, protesting that even the smallest size was too big, and took small sips, long slender fingers encircling the cup, pursing her lips to cool the hot liquid with her breath. Very cute.

To conceal my fascination with her lips I quickly complimented her English, which was smooth with only a trace of an accent.

"My dad put me in an English language school."

"So, which language do you feel more comfortable in?" I asked.

"Spanish," she replied without hesitation. "Well, if I'm talking economics, then English maybe, but about feelings, Spanish always. It's a wonderfully poetic language."

"But English is the world language," I countered. "It must have a larger descriptive vocabulary…"

Bianca was shaking her head.

"My anthropology prof said all languages have about the same number of words, but emphasizing different things," she said. "An African tribe might have a hundred words for different types of clouds, because the moods of nature are vital to their survival, but we have only a few, because we only worry about the weather when there's a hurricane. Of course, English has lots of words for financial instruments."

The girl was not only good-looking, but bright. Time to back pedal, make sure I wasn't coming over as an Ugly American, up my chances of a second date.

"I'll take your word for it since you know more than one language. Did you major in anthropology?"

She had started as an economics major, but eventually decided it really was a dismal science, and changed to anthropology. We talked for about an hour and she agreed to go to dinner with me.

I gave her the choice of restaurants, because she didn't strike me as the type who would name the most expensive restaurant in town. Anyway,

DNA Blues

I could take the hit. I was earning a fat salary at Scotia Bank, even more than I was making at Bank of America in Raleigh before deciding to go for a change of scene.

My instincts were right on target. Bianca chose a Middle Eastern restaurant on Roosevelt Avenue with moderate prices and good food for our Friday night date.

I was seated facing a bar with inverted wine glasses hanging from the ceiling, glimmering in the artificial candlelight. Bianca had a view of a display of hookahs and string instruments. The walls were decorated with paintings of scantily clad dancing girls, and a male voice wailed out what must have been a song of lost love in Arabic.

While eating falafel for appetizers, we got into the inevitable exchange about what two good-looking, charming, well-adjusted people were doing looking for a date online. Of course, the subject was brought up casually without addressing the issue head on. Bianca told me that she had gone on to finish her Master's in Social Work, and then to work for Social Services, a government office without a single male employee except the cleaning guys.

My excuse was being a newcomer to Puerto Rico. I should have had the sense not to provide further explanation, but the story of my divorce came spilling out. Not a good idea. Everyone knows the last thing you should do on the second date is go on and on about your ex.

"We were married eight years. I thought we were really in love. I know I was," I told her.

"What happened?"

"The same old story," I said.

"Every story is different."

I gave Bianca the short version of my life, explaining how the first years with my wife Pia were like a dream too good to be true for a loner like me. My parent's marriage had fallen apart after my thirteenth birthday, and I was privileged to witness the breakup blow by blow, until my mom disappeared, and my dad put me in Exeter. I'd gone on to an Ivy League

The Pinch of the Crab

university and a banking career, but coming home to a woman I loved, who seemed to love me, was an unexpected happiness. Of course, I didn't tell Bianca about the secret games and jokes, all the little intimacies, but I must have told her enough to get the idea.

"Sounds like you should never have let her go."

"Pia changed. The last year she seemed distant, like her mind was somewhere else when she was with me. You know, faking it. Then I found out. She was cheating on me."

The guy was an old friend of mine. Tim came into the bank looking for help to buy time on his college loan. In the good old days, we had both been into performance poetry, and he still was, which was why he couldn't pay the goddamn loan, while I was on the other side of the desk, making a good living to support my wife and little girl.

"He still had long hair and artist charm. Good old hardworking hubby must have seemed boring in comparison."

Bianca wasn't put off by the story of my divorce. She was sympathetic, and expressed concern about my separation from my daughter Katie.

"Your move to Puerto Rico means you can hardly ever see her," she said.

"Yeah, that's the hardest part," I replied. "But I didn't have much choice."

That wasn't 100 per cent true, but my real situation was complicated.

"That's enough about me," I said. "Tell me about yourself."

Bianca talked a bit about her family and her job. Her parents lived in Cayey, up in the mountains, and her father was a retired professor of Sociology at the University of Puerto Rico. Her younger brother Simón had never finished college. After a stint in the US Navy, he got a job in a hurricane-proof windows company and moved up to assistant manager. Brother and sister weren't close as teenagers, but after Simón's daughter Irene was born, they bonded again. Bianca said her love for her niece sometimes made it hard to work with cases of abused and neglected children.

"Do you like the work at Social Services?"

Bianca reached with her fork for a lamb kabob and ate it slowly. "It's not a job you like. I've seen some horrible things, but most of the time I believe in what I'm doing and that's the important thing."

"Only most of the time?"

"The Department is awfully conservative about removing kids at risk from their biological parents. Sometimes I recommend removal, but they overrule my recommendation, or the red tape takes too long, and then something horrible happens."

She sighed.

"Would you rather talk about something else?"

"It's been a bad week for me. The last two days I was trying to find a temporary home for a seven-year-old girl. The mother is in the hospital with terminal cancer, the grandmother has Alzheimer's. I finally got in touch with the father who had divorced the mother several years ago, but he was already into his new family, completely uninterested in taking his daughter into his home. The girl cried and cried until my heart almost broke. She's the same age as my niece. I couldn't understand a father so hard-hearted."

She shook her head. "He's a well-placed professional, a respected man in the community. I don't know how he could just abandon his daughter."

"What will you do?" I asked.

"Find a foster home, but some of them are just into it for the money."

"The little girl is lucky to have you as her advocate."

Bianca smiled and thanked me, her voice barely audible above the sudden upbeat in the volume of the drums accompanying the flute of an Arabic song on the sound system. A dancer emerged swathed in transparent veils revealing the smooth curve of her belly and a jewel in her navel. I reined in my roving eyes, and asked Bianca whether she liked belly dancing. You never know with women. Pia would have denounced it as sexual exploitation, but Bianca admired the art of the dance.

The dancer's bleached blonde hair was all wrong for the sultry look that turns me on, but she had a superb figure. I fingered the soft leather of

The Pinch of the Crab

my calfskin wallet, thinking about how the down on her belly would feel if I dared to slide in a fiver, but then again, my date might not accept the gesture as a form of art appreciation.

Bianca had come to the restaurant on the urban train, but I took her home in my BMW, bought used during my first month in San Juan to cheer me up in a strange place. The previous owner had taken care of it like a baby and it was still an awesome car.

Bianca's concern about my separation from my daughter seemed like a good omen, so when I parked in front of the building where she shared an apartment with a couple of girlfriends, I ventured a goodnight kiss. She let me kiss her briefly, but drew back before I got any ideas about going further.

"Thanks for a lovely evening, Stan."

"I enjoyed it, too. I'll call you soon."

As I slowly drove away, doubts arose. She was obviously not looking for a one-night stand, or even a whirlwind romance, and I wasn't up for more, not after the job my ex had pulled on me. Besides, it was scary how much she looked like Pia. My ex was half Italian, dark eyes and olive skin.

After a week, Bianca's number registered on my cell, but I didn't pick up. Another week went by and the boss announced a party for visiting bankers from Canada. The secretary organizing the big shebang wanted to know whether I was bringing someone. Bianca came to mind immediately, good looking, bright, and English-speaking, just the type of woman to help me impress the powers that be.

I called her and made some excuse about having been called out of town unexpectedly for a seminar. She accepted both the explanation and the invitation.

At the party, I was attentive, bringing her drinks and hors d'oeuvres, and introducing her to all the important people. She looked stunning in a silver sheath. Presenting Bianca to my immediate superior on the brokerage side felt good, especially since his wife was a dumpy woman in an embarrassingly tight flowery purple dress. The woman's only noticeable curve was the tire round her waist.

Bianca did fine in the talking department, too, giving one executive an explanation of how the economic recession had started in Puerto Rico before the financial crisis of 2008, and thus could be expected to last longer than in the States. Her remarks got me started on the weakness and strengths of the Puerto Rican economy, and the visiting big shot said he'd like to converse with me further about local conditions. The next day the guys at the office joked around about how they weren't sure I deserved a girl like that. It had been a long time since I felt so good.

I began to court Bianca in earnest, inviting her to dinner, to the movies, and even to the Bellas Artes Center, which wasn't too bad, because I had gotten used to going to classical music concerts with Pia. Bianca was into theater, and I was so mad about her that I went to a play in Spanish and sat there, not understanding a word.

She must have felt grateful or sorry for me or both, because that night she consented to come up to my apartment for the first time. I had spent so many weeks being a gentleman that I'd almost forgotten all those moves perfected since the breakup with Pia. You gotta strike a delicate balance between masterful male and tender lover if you want to score. Trouble is, when you really want a girl, it's hard to remember the script.

Maybe it was better that way. There were a few awkward moments like when I pulled her on top of me in the recliner in front of the TV. We got into such a furious rhythm that the goddamn chair almost toppled over backward, but by that time we were in so deep nothing mattered. She dragged me down on the rug and we kept going. Then we took a breather and went into the bedroom for the second act.

We lay side by side, naked and exhausted, while I touched the soft skin of her belly, imagining a sparkling diamond nestling in her navel. I let my hand wander slowly to caress tendrils of hair, working my way slowly down, wondering whether we were both up for a third round, but her attention was on the family pictures on the bureau.

The Pinch of the Crab

"Is that you with your dad?" she asked.

"Yeah, at my college graduation."

"That's your mom?"

"No, she wasn't there."

"Oh Stan, I'm sorry," said Bianca. She had already told me her own mother called every day while she was at college.

I shrugged. "Her loss."

"Was she ill or something?" asked Bianca.

I told her my mother had gone to California, and developed a career, guiding women in physical and spiritual exercises to get them in touch with their inner female strength, or something like that, but Mom didn't get in touch with me more than once a year.

"Stan, you can't be serious. That's awful."

"Yeah, I remember the other guys at Exeter getting calls and care packages." I shrugged. "It hurt, but I'm used to it now."

Bianca reached out and stroked my head gently. My eyes got teary. She kissed me and said, "Do you have a picture of your daughter? I'd love to see it."

I got up and opened a drawer to scrimmage through a pile of second-best photos, the ones that didn't get into Pia's yearly albums. Like an idiot I hadn't thought to put up a photo of my daughter before inviting a child welfare social worker into my home. But why in hell did Bianca have to pry? Sure, she was being the perfect girlfriend, sweet and caring, but all I wanted was to be alone with her and forget the world outside.

I could feel Bianca's eyes boring into my naked back while my hands flipped through photo after photo of me drinking with my buddies on a boat. Finally, I found an old snapshot of Katie learning to ride a bike, sitting on the seat, while I held it steady.

Bianca thought Katie was adorable. "Look at the way she's looking at you. Like me when I was little. Mami still complains that I'm a daddy's girl."

I sat back down on the bed with my back toward Bianca. "Katie hasn't been close to me since the divorce."

"Stan, I'm so sorry." Bianca tugged at my arm until I turned and faced her. "Is your ex making it difficult for you to see your daughter?"

I let myself fall back on the pillow by her side. She was lying naked on her back. The dark nipples of her breasts excited me. A little nibble might get her back in the mood, and stop all this talk about Katie. But I didn't want her to think I'm one of those deadbeat dads who don't give a damn about their kids.

Bianca took my long silence for corroboration. "It's awful the way some women turn a child against the father," she said. "They don't realize it's the child who suffers."

"Yeah. The divorce has been hard on Katie."

Bianca nodded sympathetically.

"It was hard on me, too," I said. "Believe me I was half out of my mind. The image of Pia fucking that asshole Tim wouldn't go away. In those first foggy minutes after waking up in the morning my wife and daughter were still mine, and then it would hit me. Pia preferred a goddamn drifter to me. My whole life was being washed down the drain because Tim had an irresistible smile. That's what Pia's best friend said—she knew Pia was wrong, but it would hard for any woman to resist when Tim cracked that irresistible lop-sided grin. The dude had borrowed a couple thousand off me and then fucked my wife to return the favor. So, you'll pardon me if I couldn't think straight."

Bianca took my hand in hers and brought it to her lips. "Stanley, it's over. You're not with her any more. Please, don't relive the hurt."

"The bitch wanted me to give her another chance, promising it would never ever happen again. When that didn't work, she tried to use my love for my daughter. You know, Katie loves us both so much, we owe it to her to make this work."

Bianca was watching my face intently. "You think she was just manipulating you?"

"Big time," I told her, and got up to take a piss. When I got back from the bathroom, Bianca was sitting on the bed with the covers wrapped around her. No chance of a third round.

The Pinch of the Crab

"I wasn't falling for Pia's shit," I said, starting to pace between the bureau and the bed. "I gave it right back to her."

"How do you mean?"

"I told Pia, hey, we're fighting all the time. That's not good for Katie. If you really care about our daughter, consent to a divorce so she doesn't have to see all the ugly stuff."

"You were fighting a lot in front of Katie?"

"I knew it was wrong, but we couldn't stop. Finally, I had the sense to get the hell out."

No use explaining to Bianca that I made the move after the neighbors, alarmed by Pia's screams, called the police. She didn't need to know all the details.

"After I moved out, Pia called and said she was willing to divorce as long as I promised not to take Katie away from her. But I told her, hell no, forget about living it up on child support. I'm going for divorce and custody. Little Katie deserves better than to be with a slut for a mother."

"But eventually your ex got custody?"

I nodded.

Bianca got up from the bed, letting the covers fall around her ankles. I stopped pacing to let her embrace me and caress my hair. "Don't feel bad. The courts usually favor the mother when the child is very young."

"In the end I didn't fight it."

"You were probably right to avoid a big court battle," said Bianca said softly, reaching for my hand. "It could have been ugly." Still holding my fingers in hers, she raised her eyes to meet mine. "Stan, please don't let your ex separate you from your daughter. You have to fight, because it's not just your rights as a father, but Katie's right to have a father."

"It's hard when I'm thousands of miles away."

"Don't give up. Call her."

"Hold me. Just hold me tight," I said.

Bianca and I began to see each other every day. After a couple of months, she moved into my apartment. Those first few weeks were wonderful, reminded me of those first years with Pia, that comfortable feeling when you wake up next to a woman you love. It was easier living with Bianca, because she was more even-tempered than my ex, not apt to fly off the handle about small things, or constantly bitch about women doing most of the housework. Some guys think a hot-tempered girl is spicier in bed, but Bianca suited me just fine in the passion department.

Only one thing bugged me. Once we were living together, Bianca got on my case about Katie, urging me to stand up to Pia and fight for my rights as a father for my daughter's sake and my own. I gave in and let her take me shopping for a present for Katie's eleventh birthday. Before we left for the mall, she was on the phone for forty minutes talking to her sister-in-law about whatever was "in" at the moment for tweens. By the time we got to the post office, I was a basket case.

About ten days later, there was a thank you note in the mail. I read the impersonal note addressed to "Dear Stan" and handed it to Bianca.

"Doesn't she call you Daddy?"

I scrunched my forehead and examined it. "Looks like Pia's handwriting," I said, although the letters were tall and fine, nothing like my ex's bold left-slanted script.

"Why don't you call her on the phone?"

"Yeah. Good idea," I replied.

Luckily, the next two weeks were hectic at the office. A new type of software had been introduced that the supervisor was sure was superior, but, in reality, caused constant bottlenecks. Bianca saw that I was really beat and let up on the subject of the phone call to Katie.

The last weekend in August I was invited to afternoon dinner at her parent's house up in the hills of Cayey for the first time. Bianca and I had Italian food with her folks once or twice, but this was the first invitation to meet the whole González clan, including Bianca's brother and beloved niece, Irene.

The Pinch of the Crab

Bianca's mom fussed over me at the dinner table, constantly asking me whether the food was to my liking. I earned brownie points by telling her it was the best Puerto Rican cuisine I had ever tasted. Toward the end of the dinner, Bianca's brother announced that Tropical Storm Lauren had changed its track and was expected to come right through Puerto Rico in the next 48 hours. The atmosphere at the table changed immediately. Bianca's mom started giving us detailed instructions about what we should buy on the way home, urging us to finish dessert and get going before the stores closed. On her way out, she gave us boxes with candles and bottled water.

After getting in the car I said, "Don't you think your mom is overreacting? The storm is still far away. Let's wait and see."

Bianca gave me to understand that tropical storms could morph into hurricanes in a few hours. We stopped at a supermarket and found it mobbed. Bianca had made a list in the car and she carefully ticked off each item. It was not until we were almost home that she asked about how I liked my first visit to her parent's home.

"Your folks are great."

"Isn't my niece Irene adorable?"

"Very cute," I said, and stopped, fishing for something else to say about a girl who had been too shy to talk to me. "Seemed very bright, too," I added.

Bianca launched into a description of the prizes her niece had received at school, and then started talking about her new enthusiasm for baking. "Every time I visit, she wants to make brownies with Titi Bianca."

I pushed aside a memory of Katie running into the living room to bury her head in my lap, because her first batch of brownies got burnt. It had been only a few months before I moved out. Katie had just turned eight, a year older than Bianca's niece.

"Your brother didn't talk much," I observed.

"He's not all that confident speaking English."

When we got home, Bianca got busy putting flashlights and candles where we would be able to find them in the dark and filling the bathtub in case we were left without water. After all that preparation the hurricane was a bit of a disappointment, barely 75 miles per hour. The windows rattled and the lights went off, but it gave me a cozy feeling when we lit candles for a light supper of leftovers that Bianca's mom had given us.

The aftermath of the storm was less pleasant. We didn't have electricity for four days. The first day I went to work, but then Scotia Bank's backup generator failed so I had to stay home. Bianca's brother's house in Trujillo Alto had neither water nor electricity. On the fourth day, she got up early and filled every container she could find to take over to Trujillo Alto. I was left alone, with nothing much to do except brood over that cold thank you note from Katie.

About four o'clock the lights suddenly came on. I tried to reach Bianca on her cell to tell her the good news, but she didn't pick up. I turned on the TV. By that time the storm had moved up the east coast and CNN was showing large-scale flooding in coastal North Carolina, lots of dirty water swirling around partially capsized homes. My ex lived inland, but it still seemed like a sign that I should finally make that phone call to Katie.

I muted the sound on CNN and dialed my ex's number. It rang three times. On the fourth ring I sighed with relief. No one was going to answer.

Just as I was about to put down the receiver, a high voice said, "Hello."

"Katie?"

"Who is this?"

"Daddy."

There was a long silence.

"Daddy Stan," I repeated.

"Hi."

"Sweetheart, I'm calling to see whether you're okay after Hurricane Lauren."

"We're all right," she said, her voice high-pitched and formal. "Thank you for calling."

"No flooding?"

"No."

The Pinch of the Crab

"Listen Katie, darling, I'm really calling to tell you I'm sorry for everything."

There was no answer except for small rustling noises that became recognizable as muffled sobbing.

"Please Katie, talk to me. I'm your dad. I love you."

After a pause, Pia's voice cut in. "It's a little late for that, Stan, don't you think?"

In the background I could hear the sobs, at first loud, then softer, like Katie was backing away from the telephone. Then the door slammed.

"Pia, please, let me talk to her and explain."

"She clearly doesn't want to talk to you."

"I just want a second chance."

"You never called or anything, and now after three years you have the balls to tell me you want a second chance? Come off it, Stan. Are you drunk or what?"

"No. I haven't touched alcohol. Please let me talk to Katie. I called to see if she's all right."

"She's fine, no thanks to you. You destroyed Katie and left me to pick up the pieces. A hurricane is peanuts compared to being abandoned by her father. Her grades dropped, she got into all sorts of trouble at school, and began picking at her skin until she had bleeding sores all over her arms and legs. It's taken two and a half years of therapy for her to begin to act normal. You destroyed her childhood. And now that she's doing better, you want to suddenly waltz back into her life? Hell, no."

I put down the receiver, cutting her short. Pia was just getting started, but the barbs she got in had met their mark. I threw the telephone hard across the room. It hit the wall, slid down and lay there on the floor, mocking me with beeping noises. I kicked it as hard as I could, until the pain in my big toe made me stop. Then my toe went numb and the throb of pain shot up through my gullet, and lodged in my throat. I knelt down, and slammed the receiver into the floor again and again.

What was the use of putting thousands of miles of ocean between me and my ex if I was so stupid as to dial her number? And why did Bianca have to be such a busybody, pushing me to make the one call that would put me back in hell?

I got up and collapsed on the sofa. There was a roaring in my ears that almost drowned out the intermittent bleating of the phone. I was having trouble breathing and I had to put my head down to keep from blacking out, squeezing my eyes shut. When I opened them, the TV was showing half of someone's front porch swirling back and forth in a raging torrent of muddy water, floating off toward nowhere.

The floating porch on the screen had a white wooden railing like the one on the small house Pia and I had rented near Raleigh, where we had our final argument. After I moved out, Pia wouldn't pick up her phone. I could never talk to Katie. My ex wouldn't have let me in if I showed up at the door, so I left work early and went to the playground. My lawyer had told me not to talk to Pia, but like an idiot, I let her goad me into a big argument.

Pia told me to forget about custody. If my lawyer was holding out that hope, he was an idiot who hadn't done his homework. The courts give custody to the mother unless she's a drug addict.

"Don't be so cocksure," I said, my voice rising to a yell. "It's not just drug addiction, but moral character."

Katie who had been on swings, came over and stood watching us, wide-eyed. It would be a lie to say her presence didn't register, but the next moment my peripheral vision blurred, and all I could see was Pia.

"We'll introduce evidence that you will bring all sorts of sleazy guys home," I yelled, "guys who might start on the daughter once they've finished fucking the mother."

For a moment I thought my ex was going to slap me across the face, but instead she began to tremble and protest that it couldn't be me, the man she had loved, talking to her this way "Stan, you lived with me for eight years, we loved each other. You know I'm a good mother."

I told her forget the love crap. "It's not my fault you're a goddamn slut."

A dark flush passed over her face and she opened her mouth wide in a frozen grimace, a silent scream. Then she found her voice. "You motherfucking monster," were her first words.

Most of the mothers had decamped as quickly as they could round up their kids. Only big ugly Greta, whom I'd always disliked, came over and stood next to Pia, as though to remind me my ex would have a witness.

Pia left off screaming at me, and wept, her low-pitched sobs alternating with the shriller cries of little Katie clinging to her skirt. Greta gave me a look and led the two of them away.

Afterwards, I sat down on a park bench next to a kid reading a comic book. It was a beautiful clear day in early September, the wooded area beyond the fence was a lush green, and the sun was warm on my back. For the first time since the whole nightmare began, I had managed to turn the tables on Pia, make her suffer the hell she had put me through. Hey, I'm not a vindictive guy, but it felt good.

On a bush on the other side of the paved path, an enormous yellow and black caterpillar was slowly making its way along a branch. The kid beside me whistled, and went over to inspect. First, he gently coached the caterpillar onto a large leaf, and then placed his cargo on the ground, raised his foot and squashed it.

"What did you do that for?"

The kid shrugged, picked up his comic book, and walked away.

I got up after a few minutes and left the park.

The next day's meeting with my lawyer, Ed Davenport, in downtown Raleigh, didn't follow the script in my mind. Ed advised against trying to portray Pia as an unfit mother because of one affair.

"Unless the judge is very old-fashioned, we'd have to prove a repetitive pattern of immoral behavior to make it stick," he said.

"Look," I told him, "I want a lawyer who will fight. The bitch has screwed me over and I don't want her doing it a second time in court. Let me know if you've got what it takes, or let me get another lawyer."

My truculence didn't faze Ed. He put his elbow on the smooth mahogany of his giant desk, cupped his chin and stared at me like I was a trapped raccoon, thrashing about needlessly. He told me in a slow deliberate tone that I was getting one of the best divorce lawyers in the state at a bargain price because we had been together at Exeter. If I didn't want to get fucked over by Pia's lawyer, I had better forget the emotional fireworks and listen carefully to every word, because he was the best in the business.

Ed advised a compromise with generous visitation rights for me. If we sue for custody, and make hostile allegations, it could backfire. He would negotiate with Pia's lawyer to get an agreement with generous visitation rights for me and reasonable child support payments. Meanwhile, I should have as little contact with my wife as possible, and above all, avoid arguments and name-calling.

"Okay,' I told him. 'I'll play it your way."

Ed reported that he was making progress with Pia's lawyer, but just as they were reaching a mutually acceptable agreement, she broke it off. Child support was the sticking point.

"You mean the bitch wants to clean me out," I said.

"The judge might see it differently," said Ed. "What your ex is asking for is pretty much in line with the amount of child support usually awarded when the father had an income similar to yours."

"No way am I going to pay what she's asking. Hell, my ex is a slut. How do I even know Katie is my daughter?"

Until that moment that thought had never crossed my mind, but once articulated there was no dislodging it. Pia and I both have dark hair and eyes. I've never been into blondes. But my daughter is very fair, a towhead with green eyes. My mother has light eyes, and people talk about genetic traits skipping a generation, so I had never worried about if before.

The lawyer pointed out that I had accepted Katie as my daughter for eight years, but I wouldn't let the issue go. Pia had betrayed me with Tim, why not with someone else? Ed finally consented to broach the issue of a DNA test. The opposing lawyer said his client was against it, and appealed to us to consider the psychological damage if the child came to know her father doubted paternity. Then, to Ed's surprise, Pia's lawyer called back the next day to say they were willing to lower the child support demands if we would drop the paternity test.

"We've got them," I said.

Ed beamed and clapped me on the shoulder. "You see what you get when you follow my advice?"

Under ordinary circumstances I wouldn't have let him get away with this shit. I'd had enough of his sneaky way of taking credit for other people's ideas when we were both in student government. But I had more important things on my mind.

Ed was thumping his fist on the desk. "We got 'em cornered, and we're gonna push 'em through the goddamn wall. We won't drop the demand for a paternity test until they drop the demand for child support payments by half!"

"That's not what I want," I said. "I have to know."

When Bianca came home, she looked at the picture dangling askew, the bleating telephone, and my red eyes. She went over, reached up a hand to straighten the picture, and then put the receiver back in place. I hadn't realized how loud the beeping was until it stopped.

"Mi amor, what happened? Are you all right?"

"What do you think?"

"Stan, darling, tell me what's wrong."

"I let you talk me into calling Katie, that's what wrong."

"She wouldn't speak to you?"

I shrugged. "I was just getting over the trauma of my divorce, but you had to go poking your nose in. Stan, dear, you have to buy Katie a present, you have to call her. Well, for your information, Katie doesn't want anything to do with me."

"I was only trying to help. You shouldn't give up hope. After three years, it's only natural she would be stand offish. Katie must be hurting. You have to give her time."

I got up and walked over to the dresser where Katie's picture was mounted in the frame Bianca had bought.

"Don't ever mention my daughter's name again," I yelled. "Butt out."

I lifted the picture up and stared at it.

"She's not even my real daughter."

"What do you mean? Her nose looks just like yours," said Bianca, coming up beside me, pointing. "And her chin…"

I slammed the picture down hard, and heard the crackle of shattering glass.

Bianca put her hands over her ears "Oh my God. Stan, what are you doing?"

"Looks can deceive. She's not my daughter."

"How can you be sure?"

"Because the goddamn DNA test said so."

Bianca looked puzzled.

"What's not to understand?" I asked. "A paternity test showed I'm not the father."

"But they can't do that to you, Stan. You took care of that little girl for eight years, loved her, walked her to school every day. They can't take her away from you."

"Yeah, but it was all a big fat lie. I'm not her father."

Bianca was watching me with a strange expression on her face. "But Stan you are Katie's father. The only father she has ever known."

"What the hell is that supposed to mean?"

"Being a parent is about love. Thousands of parents adopt and love the child as much as their own."

"Love's got nothing to with it. Look Bianca, it was a con job. Pia wanted someone to support the kid and she found the sucker who would."

The Pinch of the Crab

Bianca picked up the picture and held it out to me. "Look at her," she commanded. "Stan, for God's sake. It's not her fault."

The crack in the glass went through Katie's face, distorting her smile into a grimace.

"I don't care whose fault it is," I said, grabbing at the picture. Bianca held on tight, tugging against me with unexpected force.

"Let go," I yelled. "It's my daughter."

Her grip loosened and she watched me while I removed the broken glass, put it in the waste paper basket, and replaced the photo on the bureau, right side up. Katie's smile looked normal again.

"Stan, I'm trying to understand. Who asked for the paternity test?"

"I did. I sure as hell wasn't going to pay child support for a kid that's not mine."

"You're not paying child support now?"

I shook my head. "Pia settled for a lump sum. She said I had to choose. Either be Katie's father all the way, or get out of their lives, so I got out."

"The judge accepted that? What about Katie's welfare?"

I shrugged. "Ed's a first class divorce lawyer who does his homework. Got in touch with that Texas dude who founded the organization against paternity fraud to find out what works in court. Ed pushed the fraud angle hard—you know, Pia knew all along and tried to milk me. He was convincing, but even so, Pia's lawyer took advantage of the judge's concerns about Katie to increase the lump sum. The hardest part was I had to stay away from Katie to show I wasn't ambivalent about her not being my kid."

"When was the last time you saw your daughter?"

"That time in the park."

"You've never seen her since?"

"No."

"Did you ever think what Katie suffered? She was only eight and she lost her dad because some lab said she had the wrong DNA. She must have felt completely abandoned."

"Wait a second. What about me? What about my suffering? I was a dad and then suddenly I wasn't."

"It was hard for both of you."

"Well, it's about time you realized I'm made of flesh and blood, too. You're supposed to be in love with me, we're supposed to be partners, but all you care about is Katie."

"It's all about you, isn't it Stan?"

"Yes," I screamed, "it's about me. Even if I don't matter to *you,* I matter to myself."

"That's pretty obvious."

"What's obvious?"

"You do a real good job taking care of number one."

I walked over to where Bianca was standing and pushed her backwards with enough force to pin her against the far wall of the living room. "Say that again."

She tried to wriggle out, but I had my hand on her breast bone. She wet her upper lip with her tongue nervously, her eyes round with fear. I increased the pressure until Bianca cried out, saying she was sorry, begging me to stop.

Her voice brought me back to my senses. What in hell was I doing? I released her and took a step back.

"Can we talk about something else?" I asked her. "Thinking about Katie drives me out of mind."

Bianca nodded. She stood trembling, her eyes on the front door. I moved sideways, putting my body squarely between her and the exit. She drew back nervously, her back to the wall. I reached out and took her hand. She didn't resist when I led her toward the sofa.

Obediently she sat down next to me and allowed me to put my arm around her shoulder. I held her close.

"Mi amor, forgive me."

She tried to smile as she always did when I spoke Spanish because my accent amused her, but the smile was replaced by tears. Her cries were muted, but I could feel the violent trembling of her body.

The Pinch of the Crab

I explained to her that I was half out of my mind because of what happened with Katie, and I never meant to hurt her. I asked her whether she was angry with me, and she shook her head. I apologized again, and stroked her hair. Her body was still quivering. Finally, she muttered something about going to the bathroom. She was no longer crying when she came back, but since neither of us had much to say, I put on a Netflix movie, one of those romantic comedies with happy endings Bianca liked.

We watched the movie and went to bed. Things seemed almost back to normal between us, so I turned toward her and pulled her to me. She stiffened in my arms, and then yielded, returning my kiss, but it could have been all an act because she was afraid of me and didn't want to get hurt. I'm not that type of guy. I would have stopped if she'd said no, but she didn't, and I went ahead. In the middle when it was impossible to hold back any longer, I asked her whether she could come and she said no, it was all right. But it wasn't all right by me. Bianca was not the type of woman who needed lots of coaxing to come.

I rolled off her and said, "You weren't into it."

"Too tired, I guess," she said carefully.

"Or maybe you wanted me to feel like a jerk."

Bianca didn't answer.

I wanted to say more, but decided not to push it further.

When I woke up in the morning, Bianca was gone. Her clothes were in the closet, but her toothbrush and all her bath stuff were gone. My mouth still tasted sour after I brushed my teeth. Little Miss Social Worker had made me feel like the worst dad in the world and then she left. When the going got tough, the bitch walked out on me.

Her brother Simón came by the next day to pick up her clothes and books. He was in short sleeves, a snake tattoo visible on bulging biceps. On his way out, he warned me not to get anywhere near his sister ever again if I knew what was fuckin' good for me. It would make his day to cut the balls off a gringo creep like me.

Bianca was right about his English. It was heavily accented and none too grammatical, but he got his message across. I closed the door behind him without a word and pulled the safety latch down.

The next day I noticed Scotia Bank had posted a job opening in Malaysia for a person willing to go overseas. I was a bit over-qualified, but what the hell, might as well apply. Puerto Rico was too close to home.

Marcia and Mercedes

A blonde girl about my age sat across from me, waiting to board the plane from New York to Puerto Rico, her nose in a book. She looked like a typical American tourist, except the book was Garcia Marquez's *One Hundred Years of Solitude* in Spanish. Could she be in the student exchange program at the University of Puerto Rico like me? A flight attendant invited business class passengers to board. The girl opened a red leather carry-on embossed with the initials M and C, placed the book inside and proceeded to the gate.

Yours truly, Mercedes Colorado, was in the last group to board. I had to scramble around an enormous guy with sleeve tattoos on his arms to get to my window seat, but I didn't regret it when we began the descent into San Juan. Cloud-covered mountains loomed into view, and then the Condado skyline. My fingertips tingled, anticipating the touch of the sacred earth of my native land. Once inside the terminal, I knelt down, kissed two fingers and touched the floor.

My bag was the last to appear on the conveyor belt. I grabbed it and walked into the humid air outside the terminal. The blonde girl was already with a group of students surrounding a silver-haired lady whose dangling ID card said Mrs. Martínez, coordinator of the UPR-CUNY Student Exchange Program. We all climbed into a minivan and introduced ourselves. The girl's name was Marcia Callahan.

The Pinch of the Crab

On the way to the Río Piedras Campus, Mrs. Martínez pointed out the sights.

"This is the banking district," she said as we drove through Muñoz Rivera Avenue, studded with skyscrapers and an occasional palm tree.

"Wow! I never thought there would be so many tall buildings," Marcia said.

What was she expecting? Grass huts?

Mrs. Martínez said she liked the San Juan of her childhood better. Not so many skyscrapers then. Houses had big porches where people sat and talked with the neighbors. When we got to the student activities center, she handed out cards with dormitory assignments. Marcia came over to me and said how glad she was to be my roommate. I put on my best fake smile.

After we both had dragged our suitcases up a narrow staircase, Marcia asked, "Are your parents Puerto Rican?"

"Yeah. Born here, but grew up in New York."

"I'm a New Yorker, too."

"How's your Spanish?" I asked.

"No sé. Todo el mundo me habla en inglés."

"Shit!" I grinned. "Your Spanish is as good as mine. Hey, do you mind if I take this bed next to the window?"

"Sure."

I opened the louvers and looked out into the dusk. "I love to listen to the coquis, you know, tree frogs. Reminds me of visits to my abuelita when I was little."

"They're awfully loud."

"You don't like the sound?"

"They sound like cicadas. Sad."

I sat down on my bed. "The song of the coqui makes me happy."

Things weren't getting off to a great start. If you meet someone casually and find out they don't see things the way you do, you stay out of her way, but if you're stuck with a roommate like that, tough luck.

Marcia and Mercedes

We unpacked in silence. Then I remembered to call my mother. "Damn. There's no reception. Jesus Christ! Mami will be frantic. She's paranoid about airplanes."

Marcia's phone didn't have any reception either. "I've got to call my dad."

"Your dad's the worrywart?"

"Yeah," said Marcia. "He brought me up."

"Where's your mom?"

"She... went away."

"How old were you?"

"Six," said Marcia. She put down her phone. "That's why I don't like cicadas. There were lots of them the summer my mother went away. It was so lonely in my room listening to them. They got in the window, nasty brown things. I didn't want to go to bed. My grandmother wouldn't let me come out even when I cried. Bedtime at eight was sacred."

"You weren't in the city then?" I asked.

"No, some town in Connecticut. My grandmother wouldn't tell me what happened to my mother."

"I'm sorry."

"It's okay," said Marcia. "Things got better when my dad came and took me to the city. He spoiled me."

"Mami brought me up. Papi was in the Gulf War. He came home for six months. Then he just left."

"I'm sorry."

"It's okay. I never think about him."

The corners of Marcia's mouth crinkled in a half smile. "You know what, Mercedes, we're both half orphans."

"Right. Which desk do you want?"

Maybe the roommate thing was going to work out after all.

The next morning, Marcia was nowhere to be seen. I opened the louvers to let the sun in and saw Marcia in the courtyard below sitting on a bench. After putting on my makeup, I went down to join her. She

The Pinch of the Crab

was watching a small black and yellow bird going from one orange torch flower to another.

"Is that a hummingbird?" she asked.

"Nah. Looks like a reinita. Hey, aren't you the early bird?"

"I took a walk. The campus is so beautiful, so many flowers."

"San Juan is okay," I agreed. "But to see real beauty you have to go to the other side. Ponce. That's where Mami's family is from. Then you'll understand why it's called la isla del encanto."

"I'd love to. I wish my dad could see the island. He wanted me to go to Spain instead."

"Yeah, I guess most people would prefer Europe."

"I'm really happy to be here," said Marcia. "But it was hard to persuade my dad."

"I guess he doesn't think much of Puerto Rico."

"Oh no," said Marcia, too quickly. The dude had probably said a few choice words about why in hell anyone would want to go to some island where poor people in New York come from.

She explained. "My dad hates for me to go away. He gets terribly lonely. He never even let me go to summer camp."

"My mom didn't send me to summer camp either, but it wasn't because she couldn't bear to part with me for two months, nope, that wasn't the problem." I looked at my watch. "We're supposed to be at orientation breakfast in five minutes."

Once the semester started, I was impressed with the number of hours Marcia spent studying. We were together in a class on magic realism in Latin American literature. Marcia read everything in Spanish. I must confess to cheating now and then, using an English translation, especially when we read García Márquez's autobiography *Vivir para contarla*. The damn thing must have had six hundred pages.

At first, Marcia didn't say a thing in class, but after a few weeks she loosened up. In a discussion on whether magic realism had a future in literature, she said sometimes a writer has to push beyond the

Marcia and Mercedes

parameters of reality to bring emotional truth into focus. The elderly professor beamed.

"You really impressed the old guy," I told Marcia, as we walked down the hall, "with all that parameter stuff. But if you ask me, García Márquez pushes it too far. Writers should write about the way life really is."

"But, Mercedes, real life is like that. We hide the dark side from each other."

I wasn't buying that. What could Marcia know about the dark side? Maybe she was a half orphan, but let's get real. Her Wall Street lawyer father had provided a cushy existence, private schools and all. Papi never even called me, let alone sent a check to help with my education.

I suddenly found myself telling her, "I found Papi's number in the phone book."

"That's great. When are you going to call him?"

"I don't know. If he hasn't missed me all these years, why would he want to see me now? How about your mom? Has she ever called you?"

"No. I guess she never got well enough to call. She's in a mental hospital."

Marcia's eyes looked red. If only I could learn not to butt my nose in. "Do you want to talk about it?"

We sat down on a bench in the quadrangle under a giant banyan tree. There were groups of students all around. Marcia was fighting to get her voice under control. "A couple of months ago, my aunt Clarissa, my mother's younger sister, called me. I hadn't spoken to her for years. She said my mother was very sick with pneumonia, and was asking to see me. I didn't know what to do."

Sounded like a no-brainer to me.

"I wanted to go," Marcia continued, "but my dad always said it would be too painful for me. That's why I never went to see her."

"Never *ever*, since you were six years old?"

Marcia nodded.

"But he let you go see her when she was sick, didn't he?"

The Pinch of the Crab

"My dad was in Los Angeles on business. I had spoken to him on the phone just before my aunt called. I heard a woman's voice and asked who it was. He said it was the TV."

"Yeah, sure," I told her.

"My dad wouldn't lie to me."

Anglo girls can be *so* naïve.

"I didn't want to call back," said Marcia. "He would have thought I was checking up on him."

"So, you went to see your mother without talking to him?"

"Yeah. It was awful. The nurse said the crisis with her lungs had passed. But she had dark circles under her eyes. I didn't recognize her. My mother had beautiful hair, reddish brown curls, but the woman on the bed didn't have much hair. People always used to say I got my green eyes and curly lashes from my mother, but her eyes were gray and she had no lashes at all, just pink lids. I went over to the bed and said, Mom, I'm here. When she looked at me her eyes were empty."

Marcia was sobbing out loud. A couple of students nearby were staring at us. I put my arm around her. A pearly-eyed thrasher alighted on the far side of the bench and eyed us. Marcia's shoulders relaxed.

"The next day my aunt called," she continued. "My mom had begun talking after my visit. Her psychiatrist wanted to see me. I went back to the hospital the next day. The psychiatrist started out asking me how I liked college and stuff like that. I guess they do that to get you feeling comfortable before they spring the real question. What she wanted to know was whether my parents fought."

"Did they?"

"I can't remember much. My mother used to yell at my father a lot. The psychiatrist wanted to know how he reacted. I told her my dad yelled back sometimes. She seemed to think I was hiding something."

What to make of all this? Was Marcia lying about not remembering? It's not all that hard to remember important things that happened when you were six. The day Papi left us is pretty clear in *my* mind. When he was going out the door, Mami said, "¿No vas a despedirte de la nena?" He came back, and hugged me close, kissing me on the forehead. Then the door closed behind him and I started screaming.

Marcia was still talking. "By the time I got home I was a complete wreck," she told me. "Couldn't stop crying for days. When my dad got back, he was furious."

"But it wasn't your fault."

"He was furious with my aunt. Said she had no right to drag me back into that hell. He changed our phone number. Then he took me for a weekend to the Catskills."

Something about the whole story didn't click for me. What kind of a man would keep a daughter from her mother for all those years? And then change the phone number.

"Maybe you should try to talk to your mom again when you get back," I told Marcia.

"Yeah. I'd like to try again. But right afterwards I was so depressed I wanted to die. I begged my dad to change his mind and let me go to Puerto Rico with the Student Exchange program. It was sweet of my dad to understand. I feel so much better here."

The guy didn't sound all that sweet to me. If he wanted to bring the woman in L.A. to New York it would have been convenient not to have his daughter around. Or maybe he didn't want Marcia to see her mother again.

As far as Marcia was concerned, the man walked on water. That's the way it is when you only have one parent. Mami was my beautiful angel at least until I was twelve. That's when she started accusing me of talking back. But hey, at some point, you have to take a stand, let 'em know you are going to dress the way you want. Parents don't always know what's best for you. Mami wanted me to take the secretarial course in high school, but I told her, no way, I'm going to college. Now she's proud of me.

Marcia was wiping her eyes with her hand, trying to smile. "Mercedes, you should give your dad a chance. Maybe there's some reason he hasn't gotten in touch."

The Pinch of the Crab

"Yeah. Like he's a deadbeat dad."

I didn't have any illusions about *my* dad. Still, I couldn't get Papi out of my mind. His number stuck like a leech in my memory. The next day I started dialing, but stopped before the final digit. This went on for some time before I finally took the plunge.

Papi picked up. There was a long pause after I told him who I was. Then he began to praise the Lord, telling me a single day had not passed without thinking about me. Yeah, sure, tell me more. But his voice kept cracking, so I didn't tell him off. He invited me to come over for dinner on Sunday. My little brothers would be so excited.

I said okay, and wrote down the directions. Then I hung up, sat down and cried my eyes out. When Marcia came in, my face must have been all red and splotchy.

"What's the matter?"

"My dad invited me on Sunday. I said yes."

"That's wonderful!"

"I'm not going!"

"Why not?"

"I don't want to see him."

"Are you sure? You'll have to call and cancel."

"No, I don't. He doesn't deserve that."

Marcia kept quiet. I took out a book and pretended to be studying. After a while I said, "I'll go, if you go with me."

"But Mercedes, I'm not invited."

"It's a barbecue, not a fucking formal dinner party."

"Okay, okay, I'll go."

The barbecue went as well as could be expected. We went in Marcia's rental car, which her father had arranged for the whole semester. I got all emotional when we turned off Sixty Fifth Infantry Avenue onto a side street with lots of bougainvillea. On the side of the house, I saw Papi's name and street number: Pedro Colorado y familia, Calle Violeta 1623. The one-story concrete house was painted white with dark green iron grillwork. He had made an extension of the carport out into the small back yard to create a barbecue area. About twenty-five people were crowded onto the rustic orange tiles or grouped on the lawn under a mango tree.

Papi gave me a big hug, kissed me on both cheeks, and then welcomed Marcia. He introduced us to all the relatives, proudly announcing that his daughter and her friend studied at CUNY. Miguelito and Pedro, my two little brothers, were fascinated with the new big sister they had never met. Halfway through the evening, a tall young man, who would have been handsome if he wasn't so thin and gangly, came rushing over calling out "Mercedes."

"Don't you remember your cousin Juan?" said Papi. "Your Aunt Alicia's son. You used to follow him about like a little puppy when you were four years old."

I kissed Juan on the cheek. "Sure, I remember. But how was I to recognize you when you're six feet tall now?"

My stepmother Carmen came over, gave me a hug and complimented Marcia on how well she spoke Spanish. Afterwards Carmen hovered over us the whole night, making sure we tried the different fritters. She kept pushing us to eat and drink.

When we got back to the dorm late at night, Marcia said how much she liked my father and his family. "They're really sweet people. Your dad really cares about you. And your stepmother was very nice."

"Yeah, but did you notice she never let me talk alone to my dad? Stuck around like a leech. I wanted to slap the goddamn fake smile off her face, the bitch."

"But, Mercedes, that's not fair. She…"

"Don't tell me what's fair. The bitch took my dad away from my mother. I'm sure she's the one who prevented him from calling me. I hate her."

"He didn't have to listen to her."

"Yeah, well then I hate him, too," I said, and began to cry. The sobs were so big that my body kept shaking. Marcia sat down next to me and

The Pinch of the Crab

put her arm around my shoulder. When I calmed down, she gave me a tissue.

I blew my nose. "What I mean is I hate him for the way he acted then. Not the way he's acting now. Did you ever hate your mom for leaving you?"

"I don't remember."

"And how do you feel about her now?"

"I don't feel anything."

"But she's your mom."

"Mercedes, you don't understand. She just lies there. Doesn't recognize anyone."

"But it's not her fault she left you because, you know, she was already…"

"Crazy. Yeah, I guess if you see it that way it wasn't her fault."

"She probably loved you very much," I said.

"Not enough," said Marcia. "She didn't love me enough to stop, you know…"

That phrase could only mean one thing. Her mother drank or did drugs. "Stop what?"

"Stop provoking him."

"Who?"

"My dad."

"Oh. What do you mean?"

Marcia said she couldn't talk about it, and I didn't push it. But I sure would have liked to know what exactly her father did when he was provoked.

Next week we went over to Papi's again. This time my stepmother Carmen was busy talking to her niece who had just got back after a year studying in Mexico, which suited me fine because I got some time to talk to Papi. He brought me up to date, telling me all about what my aunts and uncles and cousins were doing. Juan, the tall cousin whom I used to follow around when we were kids had started out majoring in literature in college, just like Marcia and me, but then went for a pharmacy degree and got a job at Walgreens.

Papi wanted to know whether I had given thought to the practical aspect of education. I said law school was a possibility if I could get enough financial aid. That was as close as we got to talking about anything personal. I wasn't going to put my feelings on the line for someone who hadn't bothered to see me for fourteen years, at least not right away.

When my uncle joined the conversation, I remembered to look around for Marcia. That's when I noticed two heads close together. Marcia and Juan were off to one side, their two plastic chairs side by side, deep in conversation.

I got up and walked toward them. Marcia was tracing a huge circle in the air, making a point about circular reasoning in the fiction of Borges. Juan leaped up to get me a chair, and then took our glasses to get us both seconds of rum and coke. When he got back, the conversation about Latin American literature resumed. I could hardly get in a word in. Marcia and Juan were exploring a joint passion, intoxicated by unexpectedly finding a kindred spirit.

That first semester at the University of Puerto Rico was a special time for me. Even if Papi hadn't done right by me when I was a kid, his affection made me feel good. He said it took him ten years to get himself together after returning from the Gulf War. He kept having bad thoughts about people, like everyone was out to get him, and got fired from more jobs than he could count. Maybe, just maybe, Marcia had a point about extenuating circumstances.

Papi must have wanted to make up for all those years being a deadbeat dad, because he kept talking about getting some money together to help me go to law school. Not that I was counting on it. I'd rather count on my own smarts and my mom. We went through some rough spots when I was in high school, but Mami has never failed me. She worked two jobs for years, cleaning houses and taking care of an old lady with Alzheimer's. Papi had no idea what a lot of shit we went through after he left. But what would be the point of slamming it into his face if none of us could turn back the clock?

The Pinch of the Crab

Meanwhile, Marcia was living it up. The romance with Juan was going strong. We ran around together with a university crowd that included Juan and a friend of his who had asked me out.

For Thanksgiving we went to Papi's place for a big family dinner. After stuffing ourselves with both roast pork and turkey, Marcia and I returned to the dorm to take a nap. We were to go out on the town with Juan and the rest of their crowd later in the evening.

"I'm so full I can hardly breathe," said Marcia. "That was the best Thanksgiving dinner I've ever eaten. The sweet plantain stuffing was awesome. Aren't you glad you made the decision to call your dad?"

"You're the one who should be glad, because you met Juan."

Marcia flushed bright red.

"I can't believe you, girl," I said. "So shy and soft-spoken. I thought I'd be the first one to find a guy, but you're the one on fast track. Come on, are you two exclusive?"

"We haven't talked about it. But yeah, it's serious."

"Well, my stepmother says he is stuck on you. Goes around in a daze—Marcia this and Marcia that. I hope he's not poisoning half the population of the island by filling prescriptions wrong."

"Juan's very conscientious about his work."

"Look at how she rushes to defend the guy."

Marcia was no doubt telling the truth about never having discussed being exclusive. If you are really in love, you don't have to talk about it. The guy I was dating was cool, but it wouldn't last longer than my stay in Puerto Rico. Neither of us was serious, so nobody would get hurt. But I was worried about my cousin Juan. The guy was a sweetheart, sensitive and caring, but all guy. You don't find that kind very often. But how would Marcia's father feel about her marrying a Puerto Rican? Now that Obama got elected, people say there's no racism in the good ole USA, but give me a break.

Mami wanted me to come home to Brooklyn for Christmas, but I decided to stay. Christmas is just one day in the States, if you don't count

Marcia and Mercedes

all those days in the malls. Everyone goes to the mall in Puerto Rico, too, but the fun starts in early December and lasts through Three Kings Day. I could still remember as a child going carol singing from house to house, the non-stop partying, and all the special Christmas food, arroz con gandules, yummy pasteles and flan.

Maybe it was the presence of Juan rather than my description of the joys of Christmas in Puerto Rico that convinced Marcia to stay. Her only doubt was about leaving her father alone on Christmas. While we were studying for finals, she told me she had good news.

"My dad's coming here for Christmas."

Didn't sound like good news to me. "Great. Do you think he'll like it?"

"He's coming down to see if it's as wonderful as I say."

Papi insisted on inviting both father and daughter for the family Christmas dinner, but Marcia had already made reservations for a grand tour of the island. They would first go to Ponce to see the old historical sights and the art museum, then to Rincón, where the surfers hang out. I didn't suggest they stay with Mami's sister, Aunt Beatriz, in Ponce. The hotels and guest houses Marcia mentioned were all pricey.

When they got back at the end of December, Marcia insisted I go to lunch to meet her dad. We went to the Condado Hilton, and sat at a table with a view of the sea. Winter is the time the surf is high, and you could see it crashing over the rocks. I couldn't decide whether I liked her father or not. He was about fifty, nice-looking if you go for the Kevin Costner type. The biceps showing through his touristy looking short-sleeved shirt suggested body-building. He insisted we order anything we wanted regardless of price, and told me how grateful he was to me for taking care of his daughter in Puerto Rico. The one thing that made me uncomfortable was the way he called her Pussy Cat.

I invited them both for New Year's at Papi's. Mr. Callahan accepted at once, claiming he was tired of being a tourist. "I want to see what the real Puerto Rico is like." Marcia nudged my knee under the table. It was too late. I had already extended the invitation. Had I messed things up big time?

While we were waiting for the bill, I said I'd forgotten her Christmas present in the car. Marcia offered to go with me to get it. We started walking toward my dad's car, parked on a side street to avoid paying for hotel parking. Once we were out of earshot I said, "You already told him about Juan, didn't you?"

Marcia shook her head. "I'm still waiting for the right moment."

"Jesus Christ, you told me you'd tell him during the trip. Now what do we do?"

"I'll call Juan."

"So, what are you two going to do at the party? Pretend you don't know each other?"

"No. Just be friendly normal. Don't worry. It'll be okay. Hey, where's my Christmas present?"

I shrugged. "Sorry. I made that up to be able to talk."

"I don't really want a present," said Marcia. "But my father's very observant."

"Now you're spooking me." I opened the car door and grabbed a perfume out of the glove box. "My stepmother gave it to me for Christmas. Keep it."

By this time, I was really worried. Okay, Marcia and Juan were going to act like friends, but what if one of my kid brothers yelled out, "Hey, Juan, your girlfriend's here." I prayed Mr. Callahan had taken French in school instead of Spanish.

The party went smoothly. Marcia's dad was also a Gulf War veteran. Mr. Callahan had been a marine, and Papi was an army man. Papi hadn't forgotten his English, and they had lots of stories to tell. The guys settled down next to the ice chest full of Medallas, already on a first name basis, Pedro and George. The two of them had a roaring good time.

Marcia's dad made no move to leave until it was one in the morning. Marcia left with him. Most of the young people at the party went on to

Old San Juan, but Juan and I said we were too tired. To tell the truth, I had started drinking beer early on to steady my nerves, and I was completely wasted. Papi insisted we sleep over at his place to avoid all the drunk drivers on the road. He put Juan on the living room couch and then went into my brothers' room and put them both on one twin bed, so I could sleep on the other. I lay down fully dressed and fell asleep instantly.

About four in the morning Juan shook me awake.

"Mercedes, levántate. Marcia's in trouble."

I mumbled something and turned over. Juan pulled me out of bed. By this time my head was clearing, and I followed him quietly out of the house. The sound of his car starting up broke the stillness of the night. Once we had reached Sixty Fifth Infantry Avenue, he told me Marcia's dad had hit her.

"No! You're shitting me."

"She told him we want to get married."

"OH, NO. Is she all right?"

"He slammed the back of her head against the wall and she blacked out."

Marcia was waiting for us in the Hotel Marriott. One eye looked puffy and she walked unsteadily. When we got her into Juan's car, she was shaking so badly she could hardly talk. Juan took us to his mother's house in Vega Alta, an out of the way place it would be hard for Mr. Callahan to find. After drinking some hot cocoa, Marcia finally calmed down enough to tell us how she had escaped from the guest house.

When she came to after being thrown against the wall, her dad was wiping her forehead with a wet towel, telling her she had a bad fall. He carried her to the bed, draped a cover over her, and told her to rest. She lay still, her mind racing with thoughts of making a mad dash for the door. Stupid crazy thoughts, she told herself, for a girl who probably can't even walk. She waited for him to go to his own room, but he lay down on the sofa. An hour must have passed while she listened to his even breathing. Once he began to snore, she pulled herself slowly to a sitting position. He stirred, muttered something, and resumed snoring. Her head throbbed

The Pinch of the Crab

and the slightest movement sent a jolt of pain through her neck. She wanted to pee, but going to the bathroom would wake him. Silently she stood up and groped the side table. She forced herself to slow down, feel softly. She couldn't risk toppling a glass. Finally, her fingers closed on the leather strap of her purse. She clutched it to her and walked slowly toward the door. She stopped and listened to her own breathing coming in short gasps, willing herself to calm down. The door opened smoothly and she was down the hall and into the lobby. The clerk was listening to his iPod, jerking in rhythm. Marcia went past him and reached for the front door. It was locked.

"You want to go out?"

The young man was looking at her strangely. She wished she had combed her hair. But the important thing was to act normal.

"It's not safe," said the young man. He looked at the clock: 3:15. "Lots of crime in Condado," he added.

"I just need to get to my car. I left my medicine there."

The clerk pulled out a large set of jangling keys, unlocked the door and held it open. Marcia walked out quickly, heading for the rental car. She knew her father had the car keys, but she made a show of searching in her purse, and then looked back. The clerk was still standing there, holding the door. She turned and ran across Placita Park past the homeless sleeping on benches and up a side street. When she got to Ashford Avenue, she looked to see whether anyone was following her. Then she ran a comb through her hair, walked to the Marriott Hotel, smiled at the guard, and strode into the lobby, past the bar, until she found an alcove not visible from the front door. Then she dialed Juan.

Telling the story of her escape calmed Marcia down. When she finished talking, Juan put his arm round her. The violent shaking of her body gradually subsided. "Help me decide what to do," she told Juan, "I can't think straight." He assured her she would be safe here with his mother.

"No, I won't. You don't know him. He'll find me."

Marcia was afraid her father would go over to Papi's house, pull out a pistol and force him to tell where she was hiding. Then I got the idea of taking her to Mami's sister's house in Ponce. Papi didn't even know where my Aunt Beatriz lived, because she had moved long after he divorced my mother. It would be safe, and Juan could visit her there.

It wasn't until I drove her to Ponce that I learned the whole story. It was a beautiful drive up into the mountain ranges of Cayey, green rolling hills dotted with flowering African tulip trees, but neither of us paid attention to the scenery. Marcia stared straight ahead, and gave me a blow-by-blow account of what happened in an even voice devoid of emotion, while I drove on automatic pilot, listening to every word.

All the time Marcia and her dad were touring Puerto Rico she had been trying to break the news that she was in love. She just couldn't work up the courage, she told me. When they got back to the guest house after the New Year's party at Papi's, her dad was in a great mood.

"Now I know why you didn't want to come back to New York for winter break," he told Marcia. "People are genuine here, life is simple. You know, Pussy Cat, in the Gulf we didn't mix much with the Latinos. They listened to their kind of music and we listened to ours, but they were good fighters, you could count on them. Yeah, Pedro is a good guy."

Marcia said it was awful sweet of Mr. Colorado to open his home to her. Then her father started going on about how he'd like to retire from Citibank. "To hell with the rat race in the Big Apple. Pussy Cat, what do you say? I'll retire and we'll come down here to live."

Marcia saw her chance. Speak up now or never.

"Seriously, Dad, I'd really like to live here in Puerto Rico."

"Say that again, Pussy Cat?"

Marcia reminded him she wasn't all that happy in New York.

He disagreed. "You were doing fine. Of course, you had a rough time when you were a kid with a mother like that. But your dad always came through for you, didn't he?"

Marcia meekly agreed. Then he told her it was her bitchy aunt who had dragged her back into that mess with her mother. As soon as he got back to New York he would get a court order to make the bitch stay away from his daughter.

Marcia took a deep breath and told him she didn't want to go back to New York. She had decided to live in Puerto Rico.

That really set him off. His daughter couldn't be doing this to him, she had to be kidding. He had sacrificed everything for her, never even had a girlfriend, because he didn't want to bring someone home who wouldn't treat Marcia right.

Marcia's stomach felt funny, like she needed to take a dump. She went to the bathroom, and stayed longer than necessary. I wouldn't have blamed her if she had chickened out. The man had a square jaw that could set in a hard line. At the lunch with me, Marcia had pointed out a sign saying no smoking, but he lit up anyway. When he ground out the butt on his plate, the biceps on his right arm bulged. I wouldn't want him mad at me.

Her father was waiting for her. "You got a Puerto Rican boyfriend?"

Marcia nodded.

"Then you're coming home with me. Day after tomorrow. I know all about Latino lover boys. Not my daughter."

"Dad, it's not like that. We want to get married."

"NO! GODDAMN IT, NO." He grabbed the clock radio off the side table and threw it against the wall. It fell with a heavy thud, glass splattering across the floor. The dial said: 2:25. Marcia sat very still, making herself as small as possible, holding the orange throw pillow clutched to her chest. Everything was quiet, except for the chanting of the coquis over the hum of the air-conditioner.

Her head was violently jerked back, his hand winding her hair tight in his fist, until she promised to leave Juan and go back to New York the next day. He released her. The pain receded slowly. He was still standing over her.

"That's better. Sit up."

Marcia and Mercedes

She struggled into a sitting position. The pain in her neck was so bad she almost cried out.

"We'll buy my ticket at the airport tomorrow, Dad." She heard the sound of her own voice, high-pitched, like a little child promising to be good.

"You little lying bitch. I've given you my life. And all you want is Spic cock. Just like your mother, you're a crazy slut."

He jerked her to her feet and flung her against the wall.

A jolt of pain started at the back of her head and traveled down her spine. Her knees buckled.

A long forgotten odor filled the room. The smell of her mother's hair.

"It was like a near-death out of body experience," Marcia told me. "I was a little girl again, lying in bed, and my mother was leaning over me to kiss me goodnight, the clean, flowery smell of her long curls brushing my face. I dozed off, but I was jerked awake by the sounds of an argument."

"Where were you?" I asked.

"The Connecticut house. My mother was crying. She kept saying she wanted to go back to the city. "It's so lonely here."

"You just think about yourself," her father replied. "We moved here for Marcia, remember? What kind of mother are you?"

"Marcia's lonely," said her mother. "There aren't any kids around here."

"What are you talking about? The Wickermans have two."

"They're older," replied her mother.

"You said there were no kids."

"Kids her age."

"Shut up. You lied just to prove a point." Her father was yelling now.

Her mother yelled back. "*You* shut up. You know perfectly well what I meant."

There was a silence. The cicadas hummed and then were still. Marcia got up and ran into the living room.

"Your goddamn screaming woke her up," said her father, looking at her mother.

The Pinch of the Crab

"The cicadas won't let me sleep, Daddy," said Marcia, climbing into her mother's lap. She put her arms around her mother's neck and whispered, "Mom, don't answer back, please, Mom. Don't make him angry."

"Come here to Daddy, precious." Marcia let her father disentangle her from her mother's arms and carry her back to her bed.

"Tell me a story, Daddy," she begged.

"It's too late, Pussy Cat."

"A little song? So I can't hear the cicadas."

"Okay."

Marcia told me she had been tempted to ask for another song. But she knew that would be pushing it. Instead, she closed her eyes and pretended to sleep. Her father kissed her lightly on the forehead and tiptoed from the room. There were no further sounds from the living room. Soon, the pretense of sleep turned into the real thing.

When Marcia woke it was dark. The cicadas were still and the only sound was the lonely cry of the whippoorwill. Then the moaning started. She tried to tell herself it was some unknown bird of the New England night, but she knew better. The moans became high-pitched screams mingled with low shouts. It was her father saying her mother's goddamn pretty face wouldn't be pretty any more when he got through. "Get away from me, I'm warning you," her mother screamed. "Give me the knife, you crazy fucking slut." Sharp thuds. Low moans, followed by sharp screams that propelled Marcia into the kitchen. She threw herself onto her mother's body lying prone of the floor.

But her mother was gone. It was Marcia's own body lying lifeless on the floor, and she was floating above, watching. Something cold touched her forehead. She was back in her own body on the floor in the guest house in Condado.

It was her father standing over her, wiping her face with a cool wet towel. "Pussy Cat, darling, it's me, Dad. You had a bad fall. Are you all right?"

She tried to answer, say something to stop him from hitting her again, but her teeth were shaking and her tongue wouldn't work. Her father picked her up and put her on the bed, telling her to rest, everything would be okay. Marcia pretended to sleep.

The rest of the story, the part about her escape, she had already told me. I have to hand it to Marcia. I consider myself to be a tough cookie, but after a beating like that I probably wouldn't have had the guts to get myself over to the Marriott.

By this time, we had almost reached Ponce. My Aunt Beatriz knew we were coming and she did everything to make Marcia feel comfortable and safe. Later she told me Marcia never stepped out of the house the whole week. Juan came to see her almost every day. He called the guest house and they no longer had anyone with the surname of Callahan registered, but Marcia was sure her father was still on the island in a different hotel. Juan asked a friend who had a New York cell phone number to call Marcia's dad's office. The secretary said Mr. Callahan would be in a meeting all morning.

I finished the spring semester at the University of Puerto Rico, but Marcia dropped out and got married. It was a civil ceremony with just me and Juan's mother as witnesses. I went back to New York to finish my senior year and got admitted to law school the next fall. I kept in touch with Marcia and Juan, but couldn't make it back to the island for two years.

Marcia came to the airport with a big belly like she was about ready to drop twins. We hugged and kissed. On the drive to her place, she told me the baby was due in a month.

We took the expressway and got off at the exit to Vega Alta. On the outskirts of the town, we entered a suburb of concrete houses with small yards filled with flowering plants. I didn't recognize Aunt Alicia's house at first, because a second story apartment had been built for Juan and Marcia.

When we pulled into the driveway, Juan was coming down the staircase, his face one big smile. After kissing us both, he carried my suitcase up, looking back anxiously at his wife as though she was in danger of falling down the stairs at any minute.

The Pinch of the Crab

We sat down on an old futon couch I remembered seeing in Papi's carport. Juan said they had bought everything for the baby's room, but were still saving up to furnish the rest of the apartment.

The next day, Juan left for work early in the morning. Over coffee, served Puerto Rican style with steaming hot milk, Marcia told me all about her pregnancy and how excited she was about becoming a mother. Then she said, "Enough about me, tell me about you. How are your classes at law school going?"

She listened attentively and then told me Juan had urged her to take some classes to finish college. His mom would be happy to take care of the baby, but she wanted to wait a couple of years.

"Let me show you the baby's room."

I admired the furnishings and picked up a panda bear peeking out from under the quilt on the crib. Marcia said she bought it because the bear looked just like the one she had hugged to be able to go to sleep after her mother disappeared.

"Did you ever get in touch with your mom again?"

"I tried. A few days after the doctor said I was pregnant. I only wish I had called earlier."

"Was she able to talk?"

"No. They said she had a relapse and died."

Marcia turned away from me, but I could see her shoulders trembling. I held her close. "Don't cry. At least you saw your mom one last time. The psychiatrist said she got better after your visit. She was happy you came to see her."

Marcia hugged back for a brief moment. Then she turned away, wiping her tears with the back of her hand, and headed for the kitchen to prepare a breakfast of bacon, eggs and toast. I ate heartily, but she only took a couple of bites.

"Hey girl, you're supposed to be eating for two."

Marcia picked up her fork, speared a slice of bacon, and put it back down. "My dad called."

Oh shit, the last thing I wanted to hear. "When was this?"

"Months ago. I still had morning sickness."

"You talked to him?"

"No. Juan spoke to him. Somehow Dad found out I'm going to have a baby. He wanted to reconcile. He told Juan how sorry he was. Juan said he would support whatever decision I made. Let me think it over, I told him. Then I got another phone call."

"From your father?" I asked, a prickle of fear tensing my neck muscles. God forbid the man was here in Puerto Rico.

"No. You remember how I heard a woman's voice when my father was in California? It was her. You were right. I was blind. The woman was his girlfriend for five years. She's only a few years older than me. At first, he was good to her, she said. Then she started to cry so hard she could hardly talk."

"What was that all about?"

"He proposed to her after he got back from Puerto Rico, but she was thinking of calling off the wedding."

"She told you that? I mean she doesn't even know you."

"She wanted to find out why I refuse to see him."

The phone call was beginning to make sense. You don't have to be a rocket scientist to put two plus two together. "I get it. The bastard beat the shit out of her, didn't he?"

Marcia nodded.

"Did you tell her what he did to you and your mother?'

"Not all the details, but I said enough."

"Marcia, please tell me you are not thinking about seeing him again, NEVER, EVER AGAIN."

"To be honest, I was tempted. Dad told Juan the only thing he wants in the whole world is my forgiveness. Those words made me feel all crumbly and soft inside. You know me—in spite of everything he's my dad. But then I found out my baby is a girl. I told Juan, no way. As far as I'm concerned there's not enough ocean between New York and Puerto Rico."

Neighbors

Dusk comes early in December even in the tropics. It was five o'clock on a Friday afternoon, not dark yet, but shadows had already invaded the interior of our small house. I could hear the shrill cries of a pair of pearly-eyed thrashers perched in the guava tree in the front yard, reminding me that I had taken down a nest of twigs and grasses built on top of the lantern above the front door.

To lighten my mood, I switched on the multicolored lights on the tree, and crooned the words of a Christmas carol, "y a mis amigos les traigo flores de las mejores de mi rosal." My family home in the mountains of Corozal had once been the first stop for the parranderos, carolers who went from house to house, picking up reinforcements at each stop, well into the wee hours of the morning. After most of the Torres clan moved to San Juan, Tío Hector kept up the tradition until he lost his job and left Puerto Rico for Orlando.

My voice quavered on a high note, so I stopped singing, wiped my eyes and told myself to cut it out. Miguel would never have come into my life if Mami hadn't moved us to San Juan, and little Mikey would never have been born. It was time to wake him up from his nap.

The doorbell rang. I had no idea who it could be. We had just rented a house in Villa Andalucía and hardly knew the neighbors. Through the

The Pinch of the Crab

peephole, I saw a blond in high heels, the young woman from across the street. Miguel had urged me to get acquainted. They look like a nice couple, he said, but I was reluctant. There were always lots of cars parked in their driveway, fancy cars, a BMW, even a Lexus. Our street was lined with compact flat-roofed concrete houses with iron grillwork on windows and doors. The homes were brightened up with tropical flowers in modest front yards, but it was far from an upscale neighborhood.

I opened the door. The young woman gave me a dimpled smile that softened the brassy impression of too much makeup.

"I'm Anita from across the street."

"Encantada. Gina Torres."

"Come on over tomorrow night. We're roasting a pig and Mami's bringing over pasteles."

"Sounds like when I was a kid in Corozal," I said smiling.

"You're from Corozal?" Anita's face lit up. "I'm from Morovis. Mami moved here when I was five. About his age." She gestured toward Mikey who had come up silently. He was watching Anita through one eye, his other hidden in my skirt.

Anita crouched down so that her face came level with Mikey's. "I've got a son your age. His name is Tito."

"I haven't seen him around," I said.

"He's been staying with Mami," said Anita, standing up. "But Omar said he can come live with us. The best Christmas present he could give me."

I guessed Omar must be her husband or compañero, but not Tito's father.

"I hope all three of you can come over. About nine," Anita added.

It was sweet of her to invite us. Besides, Mikey needed a playmate. Miguel and I were pleased when he learned to read just before his fourth birthday, and showed an amazing grasp of video games, but now I was worried about him making friends with kids his own age.

I accepted the invitation. When Miguel got home, he was happy to hear we would be getting to know the neighbors, but I expressed doubts.

"Anita was happy because the dude said she could bring her son to live with them," I told my husband. "You know, like she had to ask for permission."

"Negra, no le busques la quinta pata al gato. We don't know the circumstances."

Miguel thought everyone was a good guy unless proved otherwise. I'm not so trusting. My father left when I was six years old, never even said goodbye. Miguel used to tell me I'm a hard nut to crack. It had taken him two years of ardent courtship to break through my shell, persuade me that he would never abandon me, but he said it was well worth the wait.

The following evening, I fried a cheese empanadilla for Mikey at his normal suppertime. Miguel came into the kitchen.

"Mmmm. Smells good."

"I'm giving Mikey a holder. He won't be able to wait until nine."

Miguel came up behind to give me a hug, kissing my neck. I glanced over to see whether Mikey had noticed his father's hand cuddling my breast, but he was busy examining the likeness of Spiderman on his plate.

Miguel released me. "What about big boys? Do they get to eat a holder, too?"

"Sure, hon."

I fried up a couple more before going to the bedroom to look through the closet to find something a little dressy but not too formal. I discarded a close-fitting cocktail dress for a low-cut flowing dress cinched in at the waist, flattering to my full figure, a little too full, maybe, but my husband was a fan of the Jennifer López plus look. When I got back to the kitchen, Miguel gave a low whistle.

"Mami looks pretty, doesn't she?"

"She's a flower mother," said Mikey, reaching out to touch the blossoms on my dress.

"Watch out! Your fingers are greasy," I said with a smile to take the sting out of my words. Mikey cried easily. Luckily, he was blessed with a father who never pushed his son to be macho at the age of five.

The Pinch of the Crab

At half past nine, we crossed the street. Anita came running out to greet us. Once inside, Omar introduced himself, clapped Miguel on the shoulder, and took us over to the bar where he served Miguel a Heineken and prepared a rum and coke for me. Mikey sat in his father's lap, watching Omar warily. He was like that, timid with strangers, but in this case, I could hardly blame my son. Omar was a large man with a booming voice dressed in cargo pants and an orange surfer shirt, half unbuttoned, the thick gold chain around his neck fully visible.

"Hey, Tito," Omar yelled.

A boy a little bigger than Mikey came running over.

"Take the kid outside," said Omar, "but don't go in the street. Got it?"

"Come on," said Tito, addressing Mikey.

My son looked at me doubtfully, but I smiled and nodded. He followed Tito through a side door that opened into the yard.

"Don't you worry, Ma'am," Omar said to me. "They'll be all right. Tito's only been with us for twenty-four hours, but he's learned to mind me good."

I smiled politely, but that didn't stop me from finding out where the bathroom was, which gave me an opportunity to check for myself. Mikey, Tito and two other kids were running around the backyard shooting toy pistols.

When I got back, the guys were outside on the terrace. I joined the women in the living room. A woman with black hair and very red lipstick was feeding formula to her infant while complaining how hard it was to get her guy to help with the older boy. A girl dressed in pink, probably still in her teens, said her guy lost his job but never helped her with the children or the house. I didn't tell them my husband was different. That was not what the women wanted to hear.

"Omar wouldn't dream of helping around the house," said Anita.

"Sometimes I wonder why we stick with them," said the black-haired woman.

Anita lifted her finely plucked eyebrows and smiled. "Maybe we like what they do in bed."

Neighbors

The women laughed.

I laughed with them, but my attention was fixed on the terrace, where Omar was talking loudly about how much money he had spent on the new bar. When the conversation turned to cars, Miguel, who had given up racing when he became a father, joined in. After a half an hour had gone by, he was laughing loudly at Omar's jokes. I followed Anita into the kitchen and offered to take a plate of frituras out to the men. The guys had moved from beer to rum, and I wanted to make sure that Miguel got some food in his stomach. It had been hours since he ate the empanadillas.

"Hey, look what we've got here," said Omar, helping himself to a couple of frituras, while giving me the once over. It had been a mistake to wear a low-cut dress.

I moved away, and offered the appetizers to Miguel and the other guys. The plate emptied quickly. When I turned to go back inside, Omar had moved smack into my path.

"Excuse me," I said loudly, drawing back, conscious that his arm had grazed my breast. Miguel was looking the other way, deep in conversation with a guy with a shaved head.

"Ladies first," said Omar, stepping aside.

The trace of a smirk on his lips confirmed my suspicions. I didn't smile back, just turned my back on him and marched inside. Not much of a put down. If he was a butt man, he was getting a good view.

More people piled into Anita's small house. As the evening wore on, the men's raucous laughter competed with the ever increasing volume of salsa, merengue and Latin rock, interspersed with the shouts of small boys in the yard. About eleven, I went to check on Mikey, and found him sitting by himself on a tricycle, his face down on the handle bars, sobbing.

"What's wrong?" I kneeled down next to him to see his face.

"I'm not... a... baby," said Mikey, between sobs.

"Of course not. You're a big boy," I told him, resisting the urge to wipe the sniffle from his nose. The other boys were nowhere to be seen.

The Pinch of the Crab

"No, I'm not," he yelled, angry at me for not understanding. "I'm a crybaby. Tito said so." He cried harder. I wished Miguel had come outside with me. When Mikey was like this, he always knew what to do.

"Papito," I said, "you're not a crybaby if you stop crying."

Mikey looked up at me with his soft brown eyes, thinking it over. My heart ached for him. When he quieted, I took him by the hand and went back inside to tell Anita it was way past Mikey's bedtime and we would have to be going.

"But you haven't eaten," Anita protested, starting toward the kitchen.

"We filled up on all those goodies you served," I replied.

No matter, she insisted on serving two heaping plates of lechón, pasteles and arroz con gandules, and started on a third.

"Not for Mikey," I told her. "He'll eat from my plate."

I took my husband's food out to him on the terrace. He moved over to the edge of the bench to make room for Mikey and me. A slow number was playing, and some couples were dancing. I whispered to Miguel that it was midnight, Mikey was tired and cranky, and we should be going home.

"In a few minutes," Miguel replied.

Omar came up behind us and clapped Miguel on the back. "Oye, bruddah. Don't go away. The party is just heating up."

It was scary. The man wasn't there a second before, and then he appeared out of nowhere. I whirled and give him an icy stare.

Omar smiled at me, the same smirk he cracked after colliding with me accidentally on purpose. Then he put on a high little-boy voice. "Missie, this here's my pana. You canna take my buddy away from me."

I was mad, but I kept quiet. Omar's words were slurred, so I figured it would be better to wait until his attention focused on something else. Anita came out, doing a few fancy salsa moves, her hips swaying, challenging her guy to dance. When Omar took the bait, I seized the chance to renew my entreaties to Miguel to go home. He nodded but made no move to get up. We watched Omar and Anita twist and turn as the beat became faster, their bodies moving together and then apart, provoking each other to frenzied twirls until they collapsed against each other. Everyone cheered as the number ended.

Miguel finally stood up. "Just one dance," he told me.

My husband wasn't in Omar's class, but he was a good dancer. I tried to let myself go, enjoy the music and the man I loved, but the way Miguel was leaning into me, unsteady on his feet, made me uneasy.

When we sat down, Omar poured more rum into Miguel's glass. They were drinking it straight. Mikey had started crying again.

"Mijo don't cry," said Omar.

Mikey clung to me.

"Those boys bothering you?"

Mikey said nothing, just tightened his grip on my skirt.

"Hey," said Omar, "Tito give you any trouble, you let me know. I'll give him something he won't forget."

"I wanna go home," said Mikey.

I got up. Miguel was watching the dancers. I touched him on the shoulder, made him look at me. "Mi amor, escúchame, vámonos a casa. It's late."

"Sweetheart, you go ahead. I'll be along in a few minutes."

I hesitated. Omar had gotten Miguel drunk or he wouldn't behave this way. But I couldn't do anything about it short of turning into a drama queen, making a major scene, and about what? Letting my husband have a little time out with the guys.

"Don't you trust me, sweetheart?" said Miguel.

"Always," I said, and gave him a quick kiss.

I'd eaten a lot of fried stuff and my stomach felt queasy as I crossed the street with Mikey. Once my son was in bed, I sang him a couple of Christmas carols and then curled up beside him, watching him twitch and mutter in his sleep, as though reliving whatever the boys had done to make him cry. I woke up with cramps and barely made it to the john. The clock said 2:15. Where was Miguel? I called his cell phone, but gave up when it rang from our bedroom. I switched on the child monitor before marching over to Anita's house.

The music was still on full blast, but the crowd had thinned out. Nobody was dancing anymore. The girl in pink, the one whose guy lost his job but never helped around the house, was trying to wake up a man with a tattoo snoring loudly on the sofa. Miguel wasn't in the living room or on the terrace.

I found Anita in the kitchen doing dishes with an older woman who wiped her hands on a dishtowel and said, "That's enough for tonight. I'm about to fall asleep on my feet."

"Go lie down, Mami, I'll finish up," said Anita. "Omar hates to wake up in the morning and see the house all dirty."

"Where's Miguel?" I asked her.

"Did you look on the terrace?"

"I looked everywhere," I replied. "Didn't see Omar either."

Anita followed me back out to the living room. Together we checked the yard and then the bedrooms, just in case the guys were sleeping it off, as Anita put it. No luck. Back in the living room I asked the people who were still lounging around. The girl in pink, who was trying to wake up her tattooed boyfriend, said they had gone to get more beer.

"At three in the morning?"

"You don't know Omar," said the girl in pink. "But I do. He believes in partying 'til dawn."

Anita said, "Let's look outside."

Once we had entered the carport, she told me in a whisper. "What a first class bitch. Doesn't miss a chance to remind me Omar was hers first."

Obviously, Anita was more concerned about her husband's previous girlfriends than his disappearance. Maybe she was used to the disappearing act, but I wasn't.

"What happened to the Lexus that was parked over there?" I asked.

"You're right, it's gone," said Anita. "They must have taken it on a joyride."

The tattooed guy who had been asleep on the sofa stuck his head out the door.

"Damn," he said. "Los hijos de puta left without me."

"Do you know where they were going?" I asked him.

The guy didn't answer. He went back inside. I followed, determined to get an answer out of him, but the he collapsed on the sofa next to his girlfriend and started snoring.

"Please," I said, addressing the girlfriend. "Could you ask him where my husband and Omar were going?"

"He don't know nothin'," said the girl. "He's been asleep."

I waited around for a while and then asked Anita to call Omar on his cell.

"Why don't you call Miguel?" she said.

"He left his cell phone at home."

Anita started to dial, but stopped midway. "He doesn't like me checking up on him."

"For God's sake," I screamed, "it's 3:30 in the morning. They could be in some sort of trouble." I grabbed the phone out of her hand. "Give me the number."

"No," said Anita, trying to get it back. She was shorter than me, and I held it up high.

"What's the number?"

She hesitated and then slowly told me the number. At the time I didn't question whether she was giving me the right one. It rang for a long time.

"He's not picking up," she said. "Don't worry. They'll be back soon."

A high-pitched wail came from the child monitor. I stood still, not knowing what to do.

Anita looked at the child monitor and said, "Mikey must be scared alone." I took the hint and started toward the door.

"My phone," she reminded me.

I gave it back and started across the street.

The Pinch of the Crab

"Don't worry, Gina," she yelled. "I'll call you first thing when they get back.'

Mikey had fallen asleep again. I went to my own bedroom, changed and lay down on my side of the bed, facing away from where Miguel should have been. I stared at the street light and listened for the sound of his key in the door.

At six o'clock the doorbell jerked me awake. The first rays of sunlight were filtering through the Venetian blinds. He must have forgotten his key. I ran down the hall in my night shirt, ready to hug Miguel tight, cover him with kisses and scream at him for giving me the most awful scare of my life. You goddamn bastard, I love you so much, how could you do this to me?

There was a young policeman at the door.

"Are you the wife of Mr. Miguel Flores?"" he asked, his tone guttural, as though he hadn't cleared his throat, his eyes focused on the white orchid hanging from a pot on the porch.

I nodded.

"Your husband is badly injured. I've come to take you to San Jorge hospital."

"Give me a minute."

I ran back into the house, got dressed, and scooped Mikey up in my arms. The policeman agreed to drop him off at Mami's place, just five minutes away. Mikey fell asleep again on the way over.

Once we had dropped Mikey off, it started to drizzle. I asked the policeman, "Was it a bad accident?"

The officer didn't answer right away. I started a silent prayer.

"It wasn't an accident. We think it might have been a carjacking."

The pit in my stomach was growing. I tried to keep praying, but the words wouldn't come. The drizzle had turned into a steady rain. The policeman was driving very fast. A car cut into our lane, and he slammed on the brakes, throwing me forward. My head hit the glass partition. At the time it didn't hurt.

"Sorry," said the policeman, bringing the car under control. "Some idiot on his cell phone."

We drove in silence until he pulled up at the hospital.

"He'll be okay, won't he?"

The policeman turned toward me without looking at my eyes. His badge was shiny, the upholstery was covered in yellowing plastic and there were smudges on the front window left by a faulty windshield wiper.

"I don't know how to tell you this, Señora. Your husband is dead."

I had known it all along, from the moment the policeman appeared in my doorway, and spoke those first halting words. Running into the house, pulling on my clothes, making arrangements for Mikey, climbing into the police car, and rushing through the morning traffic was all a charade to prolong the time that I could hope and pray to God that Miguel was alive.

The next day a detective came to talk to me. Mami brought him into the room. He was very polite, saying how sorry he was for my loss, expressing concern for my young son. Still groggy from the heavy dose of tranquilizers that got me through the night, I had to will myself to concentrate on his words, try to make sense of what he was saying. Miguel had been found several yards from the car, bleeding from two gunshot wounds, one that exited the shoulder, and another that lodged in his intestines.

"It was probably one of those expandable bullets, you know, the kind the drug lords use. Pardon my saying so, Señora, but there was a lot of blood. It's a miracle he could get out of the car."

Grogginess gave way to a painful tightness in the back of my throat that wouldn't let me breathe. Instinctively, I put my head down. The blackness clouding my vision receded with each gulp of air.

The officer was still talking. "He was trying to go for help."

Fighting for his life, Miguel had dragged himself out of the car, gone as far as he could. He loved me, and he fought for his life, so he could come home to Mikey and me. But he couldn't go very far because his intestines were ripped open and blood was gushing out, like a flood carrying him away from us.

The Pinch of the Crab

"The other guy made it to the hospital," said the detective. "Two blocks away. He was shot, too, but not so badly injured."

By this time the fuzziness in my head had cleared. "What I don't understand is why the hospital didn't send an ambulance to pick up my husband? He was left there to bleed to death."

"According to the hospital, your husband's friend never mentioned that there was a guy with him in the car."

"He wasn't Miguel's friend."

"How long did your husband know Omar Vázquez?"

"He met him for the first time that night."

"He meets this guy for the first time, and goes out with him at three in the morning?"

"You don't understand. Miguel loves cars. He gave up racing when he became a father. It was a Lexus sports model."

The detective looked unconvinced. He got out a handkerchief to wipe his face. I didn't like the direction the whole conversation was taking. The detective hadn't mentioned doing anything to find out who killed Miguel.

"Do you have a suspect?" I asked.

"We're still investigating," said the detective. "Look, I'm sorry, but I need to ask you some routine questions. Did your husband do drugs?"

"No. Never."

"Mira, señora, it would help us find the killer if you would just be honest with us."

"I am being honest. He never did drugs even in college. Much less now he has a wife and son. We do everything as a family. He doesn't even go out with the guys." I stopped, aware that I was talking in the present tense.

"It's something we have to ask," said the detective.

"And this Omar character, have you asked him whether he does drugs?"

"He's still in the hospital."

"He's not unconscious, is he?"

"We don't have to ask him. He has a record as a drug dealer. What I'm trying to find out is what part your husband played. He was driving the car."

Neighbors

The policeman stopped abruptly to take a call on his cell. "I'll be right there," he said into the phone, got up and walked to door. Before closing it behind him he turned and said, "Gotta run. It's an emergency. Thanks for your cooperation, Señora."

I stared at the closed door. What in hell did he mean about Miguel playing a part? The detective himself had said Omar had a record. Omar was the one pulling the strings, getting Miguel to drive, hoping to throw some rival dealer off the scent. It was so obvious. But the detective didn't seem to get it.

When Mami came back into the room, I was sobbing.

"What is it?"

"Mami, Miguel bled to death, trying to crawl to get help. Oh my God, why didn't I check to see he had his cell phone before we left home? He couldn't even call."

"Mija, it's not your fault."

"They're trying to pin it on Miguel, say he was mixed up in drugs."

"They have to look at that angle."

"Mami, you know him, Miguel is the last person in the world to be involved in anything like that."

"Mija, calmate, the policeman is just doing his job. I've lived longer than you, and the world has many surprises. You never know about men. I would have never thought your father would betray me with another woman, but he was doing it with half of Corozal."

Over the years, I had grown accustomed to Mami venting. It wasn't her fault she could never get over her bitterness. But she didn't have to paint Miguel with the same brush.

"Just because you married a son of a bitch doesn't mean I married one," I snapped.

"Mija, you're talking about your own father."

"And you're talking about my husband, the most decent man in the world. The police are smearing his name. Miguel can't defend himself. And you think the detective bastard is just doing his job."

The Pinch of the Crab

"Sweetheart, don't say that. I'm on your side, I loved Miguel, too."

Mami put her arms around me. My first impulse was to push her away, but I let her hold me. It was true she loved Miguel, but he had been murdered, made to crawl while his lifeblood drained onto the pavement, and my own mother thought he must have done something to deserve it.

Mami's brother, Tío Hector, flew in that night from Orlando. I told him about the way Omar had acted at the party and what the detective said about Omar being a dealer.

"It's sounds like the police are on to him," said Tío Hector.

"But they haven't even interviewed him yet," I said. "Instead, they come around here asking about drugs."

"They'll get to it," he assured me.

The next morning, Tío Hector drove us to the funeral parlor. When we got there the parking lot was already full. Mami was worried sick about leaving her car on the street. Carjacking and thefts are at an all-time high, she told my uncle. Miguel was dead, my son would grow up without a father, and all she was concerned about was where to park the goddamn car.

I walked into the room where the coffin was. Someone got up from the front row to make room for me to sit. The casket was open. Miguel was lying there very still in a suit, something he rarely wore. His face was very still behind a veil, like a bride.

The room was quiet, except for murmured conversation, until the stillness was broken by the rumble of the compressor turning on. The petals of the roses in the large flower arrangement near the air-conditioner shuddered and Miguel quivered almost imperceptibly. My body felt peculiar, like an electric current had entered me, and was trying to find an exit.

"Look," I whispered to my mother, my eyes fixed on Miguel.

She pressed my hand, "Are you okay? You're trembling."

The rumble of the air conditioner stopped and Miguel was once again perfectly still. It was the veil that had moved.

"They did a beautiful job," said my mother.

Neighbors

I didn't think so. Miguel looked handsome, but his hair was too neat, too smooth over his temples, where it should have stuck straight up. He didn't look like himself.

A couple of hours later we left. When we got into the car, Mami thanked God it wasn't stolen, and Mikey wanted to know why Papi couldn't wake up.

"It's only his body will never wake up," said Tío Hector. "His everlasting soul is still alive with God. Your Papi will always watch over you and your mother from heaven."

Mikey looked unconvinced, but he didn't argue. He turned to me. "Mami, when are we going home?"

My son must have thought if we could just get home, everything would be back to normal. He had faith in Miguel. Papi would escape from that place where God was keeping him, and come walking in the door. My throat was swelling up again, hurting so bad I couldn't talk.

Mami took over. "Soon," she told Mikey. "But first we have to go to the cemetery."

Miguel's grandmother wanted him to be buried in the family plot in Isla Verde, but it was full and we hadn't reserved any space. Why would we? We weren't going to die any time soon. I said Miguel always thought cremation was better for the environment, the whole island was getting covered with concrete, why add more? Mami and Miguel's grandmother paid no attention. The two of them settled on a cemetery on the outskirts of Bayamón.

We turned into a wide boulevard lined with palm trees almost like the approach to the Hotel Conquistador in Fajardo. No lack of parking. The nearest plot was filled with huge headstones with elaborate carved bases, and then there were plots with simple slabs, and further on plots that had been mapped out with wires connected to posts. No doubt the cemetery advertised something for every taste and every budget.

Uncle Hector took Mikey by the hand. Mami told me to wait, she would get an umbrella out of the trunk to protect us from the sun. I had

The Pinch of the Crab

always hated the way she fussed. Don't go out in the rain, you might catch cold, don't go out in the sun, it will ruin your complexion. I walked fast. The blue sky with scattered clouds and the heat of the sun on my head momentarily made me feel better. It certainly beat sitting in that oppressive little room, separated by a veil from what was supposed to be Miguel but wasn't.

People came over to express their condolences. Some stood shyly, uncertain how to talk to me, and others put their arms around me blocking my view of three workmen digging. Red clay soil was piling up on three sides of a rectangular hole.

While I was thinking about how to get through the ceremony, I caught sight of Anita at a distance, coming out of the parking lot. There was no mistaking her swaying walk, balancing on four-inch heels. She was with a girlfriend, the one with the baby at the party.

"Omar's girlfriend is over there. I don't want to see her," I said to Mami in a whisper.

Mami went over to Tío Hector. For a man his size he moved real fast to cut Anita off before she got anywhere near me. People were watching them, tipped off something was happening by Tio Hector's lumbering run. A murmur rippled through the crowd as the news spread that Anita was the wife of the other guy that got shot. All during the funeral people had been telling me how wonderful Miguel was, how much they will miss him. What they weren't saying in front of me is that no one gets shot at four in the morning for no reason.

I went over to Jimmy Jiménez, the Pentecostal minister, and told him I'd changed my mind. I would talk at the ceremony. After the workmen finished putting up a white awning above the hole in the red clay earth, they turned their attention to tightening the ropes around the coffin. The minister led me to a folding chair next to him, and we waited while everyone crowded under the tent to escape the blazing sun.

It wasn't until they had lowered the coffin that the minister began to speak. He talked about a young man cut down in the prime of life, a good husband, a good father, and the mercy of God. I didn't see what God's mercy had to do with it. When my turn came, I tried to tell them what Miguel was really like, what he did for his granny when she broke her leg, the way he jumped into the river near El Yunque with his clothes on when Mikey lost his footing, how he read Mikey a story every night, helped me in the kitchen even when he was working full time and studying at night, and gave up car racing because he couldn't take that kind of risk now that he was a husband and father. I kept on talking.

The workmen were standing around leaning on their shovels, bored looks on their faces, anxious to finish the day's work, but I was not going to stop talking until every single person understood that it wasn't Miguel's fault. The minister put his arm around my shoulder. I broke down and stopped talking.

We threw flowers into the coffin. The last petals were still floating in the air, when the workmen grabbed their shovels and proceeded to pile the red dirt back into the hole, covering the coffin, patting the earth down firmly. Mikey was in Mami's arms staring down at the workmen, a puzzled look on his face.

On the ride back home, Mikey told me they shouldn't have put all that dirt on top of Papi, because he wouldn't be able to get out. Mami quickly took over, and explained what death means, how it's his soul not his body that lives on in heaven. Her words were soft and musical and full of crap. I wanted to yell at her to shut up, stop the car, and let Mikey and me go back to dig him out. I would hold him tight, run my fingers through his hair, and lick every grain of red dirt on his body with my warm tongue, until he quivered, and his eyelids opened to my kisses.

Mami insisted that Mikey and I should stay with her that night.

"NO, Mami, I can't."

There must have been an edge to my voice that warned her to leave me be.

"Then let Mikey stay over with me," she said.

"Okay."

The Pinch of the Crab

I knew that it wouldn't be good for Mikey to be with me in my strange state, or maybe I wasn't thinking about my son at all. I wanted to be alone in the house with Miguel. At that moment I didn't believe in the afterlife, the soul, or heaven, and least of all in God's mercy. But I did believe that Miguel would find a way to come to me when I was alone in the house.

After unlocking the door, I could still see Mami's car outside. Impatient to be alone, I waved to her that everything was all right. It was dusk, but I made no move to turn on the lights. Outside the pearly-eye thrashers were calling to each other. My restless pacing from room to room did nothing to bring Miguel closer. I opened the closet in our bedroom and reached for his pajamas hanging from a hook and lay down on my side of our bed, drinking in his acrid sweet smell. I closed my eyes and felt the weight of his body by my side.

We used to have long talks in bed about our future plans. Sometimes, we talked about the little problems that come up in any marriage, but Miguel had a gentle way of discussing things that always reassured me of his love. It took me a while to get the knack, after all Mami and I fight all the time, but eventually talking gently with Miguel became second nature. So now I started to talk softly, reassuring him what happened wasn't his fault. I just wanted him to explain one small thing to me. Why didn't he listen when I urged him to come home? He must have heard the concern in my voice, but didn't respond. What happened, how could he have ignored my pleadings and his son's distress?

I kept my eyes tightly closed and felt him caressing my hair, saying how sorry he was, everything would be all right, would I please forgive him.

"But it's not going to be all right, Miguel. It's NEVER EVER going to be all right. You forgot about Mikey and me."

He didn't want me to see it that way. It was just drunken foolishness. It could have happened to anyone, and he never imagined the consequences.

"NO!" I wasn't going to continue talking calmly, pretending that he hadn't destroyed everything.

"You acted like Omar was more important than me," I screamed. "You were trying to impress him, show off that you can hold your alcohol like a man. And you weren't going to go home just because your wife asked you. What in hell got into you, Miguel? How could that creep, that macho bastard who was eyeing your wife, get a hold over you? The policeman wanted to know what part you played. Well, I'll tell you. You were Omar's puppet. He pulled the strings and you jumped, you goddamn bastard, you performed for him. Don't you dare tell me you just made one little mistake, but you really love me. Escúchame, Miguel, you didn't love us enough. Not nearly enough."

I thrust his pajamas away from me and opened my eyes.

"You betrayed us. You chose Omar over me and Mikey, and I'll never forgive you as long as I live."

Miguel was no longer there. Even the depression on his side of the bed, the creases where his body had once been, had disappeared.

What happened next is all mixed up, but I must have gone to the closet and pulled down all his things, because there were clothes all over the floor. Then I threw all the photos of him, our wedding pictures, Miguel with baby Mikey, at the wall, laughing as each glass shard fell with a tinkle on the tile floor. But that wasn't enough. I wanted to tear every picture to shreds. I slipped, fell heavily, and began to crawl, only dimly aware of the throbbing pain in my knee, trailing blood behind me.

I don't' remember much else about that night. When I woke up the next morning my throat was parched. I stumbled to the toilet and retched, first solids and then liquid, and then pure water until I collapsed on the tile and wept. Finally, I got up and showered. I had just begun to attack the mess in the bedroom when the doorbell rang.

At the door was a detective who introduced himself as some Martínez, Juan, I think. It wasn't the same detective that came before. This one was real young, face scarred with acne, probably his first week on the force. He told me the first detective had too much on his plate, fifteen assassinations and two crimes of passion, so the case had been reassigned.

The Pinch of the Crab

Of course, I had to explain everything again. And then he said I was mistaken. Omar had no police record. This Martínez guy almost accused me of lying when I insisted that his colleague on the force had told me Omar was a dealer. What a goddamn jerk. But that's not all. The idiot tried to sweet talk me, tell me it was best for me to forget about this tragedy, take care of my son. An attractive woman like you should have no trouble finding a new husband. I told him to show a little respect. My husband was buried only yesterday. He apologized, said he didn't mean it that way.

"Yes, you did," I screamed.

He left quickly without saying goodbye, which was lucky, because if he said anything more, I would have slapped his face.

I called Mami and she came over with Tío Héctor. I told them what had happened.

"That's what the goddamn jerk of a detective said, giving me the once over, the son of a bitch."

"Mija, cálmate."

"I wanted to hit the sleazeball. Goddamn pimply creep."

Tío Héctor shook his head. "Not a good idea to assault a policeman. Escúchame, Gina, you're a daughter to me. It's my duty to tell you the way things really are. The detective may have had ulterior motives, but he was right about one thing, your number one priority right now is protecting yourself. Your son needs you. You have to be very careful. This guy Omar sounds like a very dangerous man."

"Tío, I don't care. I'm going to call the first detective and insist he get back on the case. At least he found out something. It's obvious that Omar used Miguel as a shield. He could care less that Miguel was dying on the street while the doctors fixed him up in the hospital. The man is evil. I'm sure that Miguel's murder is not the only one on his hands. I want justice for my husband."

"Cálmate, mija."

"I don't want to calm down."

Tío Héctor let me cry. In a very soft voice he said, "Mija, please listen to me carefully. It saddens me to tell you this. The world is not a pretty place, and justice is hard to come by, at least for little people like us. We know Omar is a bad man, but we don't know what connections he has, or who's backing him. Drug lords have long arms that reach even into law enforcement. My advice, from the heart, is not to push too hard. You don't want to get in this Omar guy's way. Leave this neighborhood. Give up the house, move in with your mother for a couple of years and rebuild your life."

"No. Miguel needs me. He was a good man. I won't let his name be blackened."

"Your son needs you more. Do you want to leave him an orphan? Believe me, if Miguel could hear us now, he'd agree with me," said my uncle.

I didn't back down right away. I called the first detective and tried to get him back on the case. I went to the precinct and asked to talk to the supervisor. He promised me to look into it. Nothing came of it. I got in touch with a cousin who had connections, but that didn't lead to anything either.

For months, I cried every day for hours at a time. Eventually I took my uncle's advice, moved in with Mami and found a full-time job to keep Mikey in a good school. A couple of years later Omar was sentenced to five years, not for murder or drug trafficking, but domestic violence that left his wife permanently crippled. I was sure it was Anita, but the picture in the paper was not her.

After Omar was jailed, I drove by my old house and parked on the other side of the street. A pearly-eyed thrasher swooped into the guava tree in the yard and settled into a hollow in the trunk. I could see twigs, sure sign of a new nest. A couple with a little girl came out the front door, got into a grey car, and drove away.

I stopped going to church. Mami kept going on and on about how worried she was my soul would burn in hell, but I didn't care.

"Take Mikey with you if you have to save someone," I said.

The Pinch of the Crab

I cried the whole three hours they were gone.

When I finally went back, the minister asked me gently what had kept me away. I told him I lost my faith in God's mercy when my husband was killed. But I never told the minister or anyone else about my real sin. I had summoned Miguel's living soul to me, then stabbed where it would hurt him most, payback for leaving me. "You didn't love me enough," I told him, my dear sweet Miguel who had crawled twenty yards on his stomach with his intestines dragging on the ground to come home to me.

En el campo

Victoria married a man who loved the country. On their first anniversary, Miguel drove her up to the mountains of Cayey to eat at Jájome Terrace. He smiled when she admired the tropical oaks in full bloom, and said it was a shame that most Boricuas don't appreciate living in the most beautiful place on earth. Sure, something can be said for the snow-capped peaks of the Himalayas, if your idea of fun is losing a couple of toes to frostbite, but hey, there's enough adventure to last a lifetime exploring the lush green forests and turquoise seas of Puerto Rico.

He was always going snorkeling, hiking, or, his latest craze, rappelling into limestone caves. Luckily, he didn't expect Victoria to participate in all these adventures, but about a month after their anniversary he did urge her to go hiking with him to Coca Falls in El Yunque. She begged off, reminding him how she hated creepy crawlies. Victoria wasn't keen on insects and spiders, but the sight of lizards scuttling and slithering about really gave her the shivers. Besides, the rainforest was dark and menacing, with all those vines winding themselves around their host trees in loving embrace before strangling them in the struggle to reach the light.

When Miguel returned home from the hike, he greeted his wife with a kiss.

"Hola, belleza. You look good enough to eat."

He dropped the duffel bag with his bathing suit and hiking boots on the floor, and held her at arm's length.

"Something's different."

"I had my hair done."

Miguel gave her a look. At dinner he didn't talk much. When she asked about the falls, he said Gina and Maritere, the wives of his hiking buddies, had a great time.

"I guess I should have gone, too."

"It's okay."

But it wasn't okay, because while undressing for bed he said, "Strange how a feminist like you goes to the beauty parlor so often."

Her feminist phase at the University of Puerto Rico had lasted all of three months, and Miguel liked her to look good, but her hair wasn't the real issue.

"I'll go hiking next time."

"You'll probably be too far along by then," he replied, climbing into bed.

Victoria lay down beside him, not sure whether to cuddle up. He rolled over, pulled her to him and stroked her belly, which was only slightly rounder at this early stage of pregnancy. "Don't get me wrong," he said. "I'm glad you're not like those American feminists, ugly women with no makeup."

"That was in the sixties. They're not like that anymore."

"Give me a Boricua beauty anytime."

The next day Victoria's stepmother Iris phoned. They hadn't spoken for eight years. She congratulated her stepdaughter on her marriage, mentioned that Victoria's father had recently retired, and invited the young couple to come visit them in the country for a late lunch the following Sunday. Her tone was friendly, almost casual, as though they had just spoken a week before.

Struggling to keep her voice steady, Victoria accepted the invitation with a minimum of chitchat, and said goodbye. The receiver clattered to the floor when she tried to replace it. Miguel retrieved it and put his arms round his sobbing wife.

"What's wrong? Who was that?"

When she told him, he interpreted her tears as joy at the possibility of reconciliation. A perfectly logical deduction for a man from a family of five brothers and sisters, countless cousins, aunts and uncles, a whole tribe of Sotos, all of them good-natured and affectionate. What good would it do to explain how she really felt? Her parents' overture was gratifying after all those years, but the prospect of seeing them again was something else altogether.

By the time Sunday rolled around, Victoria had decided not to go. While Miguel was out playing early morning tennis, she started to dial their number, but stopped. It would be easier to simply not show up. An hour later, confronted with her husband's enthusiasm for going to the country to meet her parents, she wavered, reluctant to disappoint him so soon after her refusal to go to El Yunque had almost caused a quarrel.

Emerging from the shower with a towel round his waist, Miguel called out, "Amor, what should I wear?"

"Mahones will be fine," Victoria answered with a smile.

Her mother-in-law, convinced that Victoria had rescued her son from a bohemian existence, was always telling Miguel to listen to his wife if he wanted to dress for success.

"If jeans are fine, what are you doing in white pants?" asked Miguel, pulling a T-shirt over his head.

"Capris are cooler," she replied, buttoning her loosely flowing, but fashionable black and white blouse.

On the morning of Victoria's visit, Iris got up early to start cooking. It had been her idea to invite the young couple. Her husband Andrés had pointed out that their telephone number was still the same if Victoria had wanted to get in touch, but eventually he came around to his wife's view that they should take the first step. Now he scoffed when Iris expressed doubts that his daughter would show up.

"She accepted the invitation. ¿Sí o no?"

"Sí. But if Vicki didn't have something against us, she would have let us know she was getting married."

Andrés gave no sign of noticing the tremor in his wife's voice. "To my mind she was going through typical adolescent rebellion. Now she's grown out of it."

Iris went back to cooking, dicing fresh vegetables from her own garden, cilantro, ajíes dulces, onions, and garlic to make the sofrito for pollo criollo. But what if the young couple really *did* show up? Andrés had become more set in his ways, more convinced than ever that his beloved island was on the road to perdition. Victoria's husband was probably one of those upwardly mobile young men full of optimism about the new Puerto Rico. Andrés despised the newly rich, blanquitos working in banks and advertising firms, who drive through red lights invented for lesser mortals who don't own a BMW or a Mercedes Benz. But maybe the husband wouldn't be like that at all. Victoria had mentioned his love for the country. Everything would be fine.

After testing the pollo criollo to be sure it was done, Iris turned off the burner. She wandered into the living room, and put the newspaper her husband had been reading back in the magazine rack. Everything was ready. But what if they wanted a tour of the house? She went into the room that had been Victoria's, smoothed the bedcover, and opened the closet door. Andrés had urged her to give the clothes away once it was clear that his daughter had left for good, but Iris never got around to it. She recognized an old pair of white sandals that had once been hers at the back of the closet, half hidden under the long dresses. Victoria was tall and slim, and Iris was short and round, but they wore the same shoe size. When her stepdaughter first asked whether she could borrow a pair, Iris told Andrés that this was a good omen. His quizzical look made her shy away from explaining it could mean that Victoria no longer harbored resentment against the woman who had replaced her mother.

En el campo

After they began sharing shoes and accessories, Iris took Victoria shopping for a new dress for a school party without a word to Andrés. Iris was the one she consulted about problems with her schoolwork. They discovered a shared passion for the poetry of Gabriela Mistral.

Iris closed the closet door and opened the bottom drawer of the bureau. There in a plastic Ziplock bag was Blackie the bear. Iris buried her face in the bear's fur, which still conserved a faint suggestion of the scent of its young owner. She placed the bear between the two pillows, his floppy head resting on his forepaws.

After eight years, Victoria found that the drive to the inland town of Morovis had changed. With the new extension of the Expressway, it was now possible to continue many miles past the coastal town of Dorado, and turn off at the new Highway 142, a much wider and straighter road into the hills. After they crossed the mountain town of Corozal, a couple of miles from her father's house, the road narrowed and looked more familiar, with torturous turns and a canopy of flamboyán trees.

Victoria had always avoided her husband's questions about her family, but as they drew near her childhood home, she made an effort to fill him in. Her father's family originally came from mountainous Utuado, and he was the first to graduate from the University of Puerto Rico.

"So he moved to Morovis to get back to his jíbaro roots?" asked Miguel.

"Something like that. My mother hated it."

"And how about you, did you like the campo?"

Victoria hesitated. "When I was little, I loved it."

"You weren't scared of lizards then?"

"A little bit, but the real phobia came later. My stepmother shares my father's love of the country."

"They sound great. The sort of people with the courage to live by their own values."

This was a high compliment from her husband. He was happy being a graphic advertising artist, but regretted not having time to devote to painting landscapes. Victoria had no such ambivalent feelings about her job. She loved being a buyer for Cachet, a boutique in San Juan.

"That's the driveway," she said, pointing to the right. Miguel braked just in time, expertly turning the car to go up a steep incline.

Instead of the waist-high hibiscus Victoria remembered bordering the driveway, the bushes now towered over their car, their red blossoms fluttering in the wind. The car took a sharp turn and almost bumped into an old Jeep Cherokee. The house atop a hill looked smaller, but maybe it was because the trees were bigger. Her father, a sack on his back, stopped in front of the steps leading to the front porch.

"Iris, ya llegaron," he called, placing the sack of grapefruits on the ground before rushing over to greet them. He looked much the same, dressed head to foot in denim overalls, penetrating blue eyes in a tanned face framed with white hair. Victoria could see the crow's feet around his eyes, but he stood erect and strong like a much younger man. He held her close for a long time, and then, clearing his throat, turned to greet Miguel.

Iris was not far behind. She wore identical overalls. Her short curly hair had more salt than pepper now, but her smile was just as warm. She hugged and kissed them both.

"Vicki, I can't believe you're really here," she said, "looking more beautiful than ever. Doesn't she Andrés?"

Once they had climbed the steps to the front porch, Victoria's father commanded them to look back at the view. Carefully tended flower gardens gave way to valleys and rolling hills, stretching as far as the eye could see. In the distance, on the shore of the Atlantic they could see the tall buildings of San Juan, like a distant mirage. Victoria had always called it the City of Oz, although it wasn't green, but gleaming white like polished alabaster.

"Hard to believe that's San Juan," said her father. "The concrete jungle. You can't see the slums, the traffic, and the garbage from here. Distance creates an illusion of beauty."

En el campo

"Breathtaking view," said Miguel. "And your gardens look great."

Victoria's father wanted to take them right away to explore the flower beds and fruit trees, but her stepmother reminded him that they must be thirsty after the long drive.

Victoria admired the new porch, constructed on the side of the house with the best view. Once they had been seated in the living room, her father launched into a long description of getting rid of an incompetent construction firm from San Juan in order to hire local craftsmen. While her stepmother served lemonade and freshly fried bacalaitos, he told them people who say wooden houses are more vulnerable to hurricanes don't know what they're talking about. This house didn't suffer a scratch from Hugo or Georges. The trick is solid old-fashioned construction. Victoria looked away. No use telling her father that category one or category two hurricanes are not a real test.

A welcome breeze entered, and the house grew darker and cooler. Don Andrés insisted they should see the gardens before the afternoon showers. Miguel rose immediately.

"You guys go," said Victoria. "I'll stay and help Iris in the kitchen."

"It's all under control," Iris assured her.

"But I'd like you to show me the changes in the house."

Her father beckoned to Miguel to follow. As they rounded the side of the house together, Victoria could hear them talking about growing plants in a tropical climate without pesticides.

Her stepmother showed her the extension they had made to the house in the back. It was a study for her father, now that he was retired from teaching biology at the University. What surprised Victoria was her old room. Nothing was changed. Her black bear was lying on the lavender bedspread, as if she had only been gone for a weekend.

"We use it as a guestroom now," said Iris.

Victoria's throat felt tight. She turned away.

The Pinch of the Crab

Everything was going better than Iris could have dreamed. Andrés obviously liked Miguel. Victoria, visibly tense during the first awkward moments, appeared relaxed at the dining table. Miguel complimented Iris on the excellent pollo criollo. Iris explained that the trick was using fresh herbs and vegetables from their own garden.

"Oye," said Don Andrés, "the cook gets all the praise. How about the guy who works all day in the sun to produce the fresh ingredients?"

"You both deserve credit," said Miguel. "This is even better than Ájili-mójili,"

Iris looked inquiringly at him. "We don't go to restaurants much."

"Nouvelle Caribbean cuisine," Victoria explained. "De moda en el área metropolitana. Lighter and healthier."

"Oh, yes, that's exactly what I aim for, a good taste with less fat to protect your father's heart."

Afterwards, Iris served the men coffee in the living room. She told Victoria to take her cup and join them, but Victoria insisted on helping in the kitchen. They worked together smoothly, reestablishing the routine shared long ago.

Victoria interrupted a momentary silence. "How's your job at the Health Services Center?"

"Good. The new director introduced innovations to make our outreach programs more effective. I'm thinking of retiring next December."

"The long drive to San Juan must be hard on your back," said Victoria.

"The drive's not so bad now that they put in the new highway. Of course, your father hates it," Iris said, her voice lightly mocking yet affectionate. "He sees the new road as a long tentacle of concrete radiating out of San Juan."

"Sounds just like him," replied Victoria. "But he only went in twice a week to give classes, so the long drive wouldn't have affected him."

"My back's better." Iris smiled. "I had therapy six months ago."

"Did you know my mother had to be operated for a slipped disc?" said Victoria.

En el campo

Iris turned off the kitchen faucet. In the five years she lived with them, Victoria had rarely talked about her mother.

"No. Your father never mentioned it."

"He thought she was faking," said Victoria, curling her lips into a mirthless smile. "He said it was just a ruse to get him to go back to San Juan."

Iris kept quiet, uncertain what to say.

"Or course, when we moved to San Juan, the doctors took an MRI and operated. Then within a year she was diagnosed with cancer."

"I'm sorry," said Iris. "Victoria, it's hard for me to say this. I met your father *after* your parents separated."

Victoria shrugged. "The way they fought it was pretty clear they didn't need a third party to come between them."

Iris felt the need to talk more, clear up any misconceptions Victoria might have, but Andrés chose this moment to bellow out that the women should forget the dishes and join them. "Just a sec," Iris called out drying her hands on the dishtowel. She took out the flan from the fridge.

Victoria was not sorry that her father had interrupted the talk about her mother. She picked out dessert plates and forks to serve the flan and followed Iris out to the living room.

Andrés got up from the cane and thatch rocking chair made by a local craftsman to offer it to his daughter.

"It was always her favorite," he told Miguel, settling himself down next to Iris on the sofa.

While Iris sliced the flan on the coffee table, passing the plates to Victoria to serve, Miguel resumed talking about the hikes he had taken with his buddies. Andrés responded enthusiastically, recounting the adventures of his youth, exploring those same caves without all the modern rappelling equipment.

The Pinch of the Crab

Victoria rocked in what had once been her special chair, and listened to the men's conversation rising and falling against the background of the coquis, whose chanting had grown louder once the afternoon turned cloudy. Her father had really taken to Miguel.

"Do you ever get Victoria to go hiking with you?" her father was asking.

Miguel shook his head. "It's hard to even get her to walk to La Coca Falls at El Yunque."

"I could never instill in her a love of the country," said Andrés.

"I liked the country when I was little," Victoria put her foot down to slow the rocking of the chair.

Iris placed her hand on her husband's arm, but his gaze remained fixed on Victoria. "You never liked the country. Your stupid lizard phobia blinded you to the beauty of nature and there was nothing I could do about it."

"Andrés," Iris said quickly. "A phobia by definition is something the person can't control. Maybe something happened that neither you nor Victoria even remembers. It's not her fault."

"I didn't say it was her fault."

"It's OK, Papi," said Victoria. "Let's talk about something else."

"Good idea," said Miguel.

"No," said Andrés. "Iris said I was blaming you, Vicki. I've got to set things straight."

Victoria didn't look at her father. Her gaze was fixed on something outside the window, her eyes moist. Her father had not lost the knack of reducing her to tears with a few choice words. But she was no longer a child, and she wouldn't let him.

"It's okay, Don Andrés," said Miguel. "You don't have to explain. Victoria understands you don't blame her."

Victoria lifted her chin and sat up straight. "No, I'm not sure I do."

"I don't blame you for hating the country," her father told her, "because that's what you were taught." He turned to Miguel. "All her mother ever thought about was her hair and nails."

En el campo

Her stepmother's remonstrance could barely be heard. "Andrés, please."

Victoria had stopped her chair from rocking, but the room was still swaying, reminding her of a small earthquake long ago, the one she alone had felt, although her parents read about it the next day in the paper. She looked at the ceiling fan. The blades were still. Her body was doing the trembling.

"It's easy to blame the dead," she said, looking straight at her father, aware of the tremor in her own voice. "They can't tell their side of the story."

His steely blue eyes didn't waver. "Don't tell me your years at the University have made you a postmodernist. One of those people that don't believe in objective truth, only different sides of the story. Your mother despised nature and passed on her narrow-minded prejudices to you." He paused. "Her death doesn't alter that truth."

"My mother had nothing to do with it," Victoria said, in a loud voice, high-pitched to her own ear. "Iris is wrong. I have a very clear memory of the childhood trauma that sparked my so-called lizard phobia. So do you, Papi."

"I have no idea what you're talking about."

"I told you."

"Oh that," said her father with a shrug.

Her stepmother looked from one to the other. "What are you talking about, Vicki?"

"Iris," said her father, a note of warning in his voice.

"Of course, if you'd rather not talk about it," said Iris, addressing her stepdaughter.

"I'm not the one who doesn't want to talk about it."

Miguel looked at his watch and stood up. "Vicki, mi amor, we have to get back." He turned to Iris. "It was a lovely meal. We had a great time."

Victoria rose, too. Better to take the escape route offered. But when her father stood up and extended his hand to Miguel, she gagged, a bitter taste invading her mouth. She took a deep breath and sat down again.

The Pinch of the Crab

"Wait just a moment, mi amor," she said to her husband. "Iris wants to know the source of my childhood trauma. It won't take but five minutes to explain."

"Querida, are you sure you want to talk about it?" asked Miguel.

"Yes."

Miguel sank back into his chair, and her parents followed suit, all three waiting in silence while Victoria struggled to find the right words.

"There weren't as many houses around in those days," she told them, her voice low but clear. "Don Cheo, his wife Doña Ines and their six children, later seven, were our closest neighbors. My special friend was Wanda, their oldest girl. She had an older half-brother. He stayed with them off and on, whenever Don Cheo's first wife was in drug rehab."

Her voice sounded flat. Her father's call for objective truth inhibited her from shaping into words subtle memories of sensation and emotion. Don Cheo was a farmer who did odd jobs for others who had more money, a gaunt man of few words. Their house was small and dark with a musty odor mixed with the rich smells of asopao cooking on the stove. His wife Doña Ines had a deeply lined face at the age of forty, but she had a ready smile, and always welcomed Victoria to her home. Awake before dawn, she was never idle, her house scrupulously neat and clean in spite of the constant flow of children and relatives.

Victoria's family was invited every year for Thanksgiving. Her father wasn't enthused about a holiday that he considered a cultural imposition from the States, but Don Cheo and Doña Ines prepared a true Boricua feast, complete with roasted pig and batata. The first time she saw the pig's head revolving on the spit, Victoria began to cry. She never lived down her reputation for being a wimp. Wanda told the story every Thanksgiving. Victoria didn't try to explain that it was not just sympathy for the pig, but guilt because the sweet smell of the meat made her feel hungry at the same time.

Victoria couldn't put all this into words. It was painful enough to lay out the bare bones of the story. Fixing her eyes on Iris, she continued.

En el campo

"Wanda's half-brother's name was Juan Carlos—Juanky, for short. He was about two years older than Wanda and me. I was afraid of him and his friends. They played rough. But I didn't have any other friends, so I spent a lot of time at Wanda's house. One day they wanted to play truth or dare. If you didn't answer a question truthfully, you had to take off an item of clothing. Wanda took off her blouse."

Victoria remembered how her friend had giggled. It was Victoria's turn next. The question was whether she had ever felt herself down there. She made a face and said no. Juanky laughed and called her a liar. Everybody does it. Feeling the heat rise from below her belly up to her cheeks, Victoria refused to admit it. The others began to chant, "Liar, liar, take it off, take it off."

"I wouldn't do it," she told her parents and Miguel. "They said I was a spoilsport. Then Juanky told his friends to hold me down. I don't know what would have happened if Doña Ines, who was pregnant again, hadn't come back from the clinic sooner than expected."

"Did you tell your parents?" asked Miguel.

"I told my mother. She went over and talked to Doña Ines who told her that Don Cheo would see they got what they deserved. Papi never talked to Don Cheo."

"Don Cheo is an honorable man," said Andrés, who had been looking out the window. "I trusted him to do the right thing."

Victoria shrugged. "But it got worse afterwards. Juanky blamed me for the beating, and didn't lose a chance to get even. He and his friends threw stones at me, followed me, threatened to come get me in the dark. It got so bad that my mother took me out of public school in the country and put me in María Reina for girls, not too far from her work in San Juan."

Victoria paused and turned to her stepmother. "Papi's a great believer in public education. Only stuck-up people like my mother, people who think they're too good for simple country folk, put their children in private school."

"I never said that," her father objected.

"Please let me finish."

"Mira, there are bullies in public school and bullies in private school. I wanted you to learn to stand up to them."

Victoria turned to her husband. "Vámonos, mi amor. They don't want to hear the rest of the story. The truth is not welcome here."

"I do want to hear. Very much," said Iris.

Her father said nothing.

Victoria gripped both arms of her chair, her fingernails digging into the wood, and continued.

"After coming home from school, I never went anywhere. It was safer to stay inside the house. Wanda came over one afternoon and asked me to go swimming with her, but I claimed to have too much homework. Then Wanda told me Juanky had left for San Juan to rejoin his mother who had just gotten out of Hogares Crea rehab."

Victoria paused. No use going into her premonition that something was fishy. Not that it mattered, because she had ignored her instincts. It was a hot day in April and she was lonely. Her mother was busy getting some paperwork for her job done, and her father had gone to get some new seedlings. She got into a bathing suit and went down the country road, hand in hand with Wanda. There was only one cottage on the way, owned by city people from San Juan, who only came on holidays. The kind of people her father said were responsible for running up the prices of real estate in rural areas, making it difficult for local people to buy their own homes. Their car wasn't in the driveway.

The road faded into a path that led down to a gully with a brook that was the favorite swimming hole for local kids. The two girls walked down the path through a meadow with high grass on either side. Victoria could hear the occasional roar of a car passing on the main road above, but as they descended through the long grass there was only the chirping of crickets and the buzzing of bees. Soon they were in the woods at a small creek. Because of the April drought, the water was too low to really swim, but they splashed about in the shallows, giggling and having a good time.

Victoria submerged her head to see a big fish lurking under the rocks. When she lifted her face out of the water to call Wanda over, she saw him.

Victoria was called back to the present by her stepmother's voice. "And then what happened?"

"We went swimming. Juanky and his two friends showed up. Maybe Wanda lied to me or maybe she didn't know he had come back. The boys started skipping stones in the water, always in our direction. One hit me in the head. I got out of the water when another one hit me on the cheek. Then they started hunting lizards, the little green ones that puff out their throats. They put them on their ears. Wanda thought this was hilarious and let them put the lizards on her ears. I said no, but they didn't listen."

Victoria stopped. What happened next was a jumble of images and sensations that she didn't want to remember, much less put into words. The boys were holding Victoria down and putting the lizards' mouths onto her ears. She was screaming, her body writhing. Wanda told them to leave her alone. They let her up. She must have looked ridiculous jumping up and down trying to shake the lizards off, not daring to touch them with her hands. The three boys rolled on the ground in laughter. Finally, Juanky took them off her. She started to run up the path, her legs buckling beneath her as she tripped on the root of a tree.

The three boys and Wanda were right behind. Juanky came over, and gracefully extended his hand to help her up, a lord coming to the rescue of a lady. Victoria said thanks. He smiled, and said he didn't know she was so scared of lizards. She told him that it was okay. But he replied that it wasn't okay. She needed to get over it.

Fear made a prickle travel up the nape of her neck. From the deep shade of the woods, she could see an opening to the sunny meadow a few yards above. But what was the use of making a dash for it when the only house near enough to hear her shouts was empty?

Victoria's father got up from his chair.

"He's going to the bathroom," said her stepmother.

The Pinch of the Crab

They waited in silence. In spite of the cool breezes coming in through the window, Victoria could feel the sweat dripping down her back.

After a few minutes her father returned and settled back down in his chair. He drained the last drops from his coffee cup, and then sat still, not looking at his daughter, gently rubbing his finger on the rim of the cup.

Victoria finished her story quickly.

"Juanky pulled out a knife, and said he was going to help me get over my fear of lizards. He grabbed a big one, the kind that looks like a small iguana with blue stripes down its sides, and told me to slit open its belly. I refused. Then he grabbed me and told me to do it or he would cut my wrist. We'll see whether your blood is the same color, he told me. Make her cut off its head, said one of his friends. Wanda told me to go ahead, giving me a look that said I had better go along. It's nothing, she said. I did it and the lizard kept walking without its head. That's all. I screamed for a while. They laughed and let me go home."

Iris had been listening intently. It was clear to her that the story was a crucial part of the past. She winced when Victoria got to the climax of the tale, and then looked over at her husband for his reaction. He put his coffee cup down. Iris got up and put her arms around her stepdaughter.

"Not much of a story," said Victoria.

"It certainly explains your lizard phobia."

"No, it doesn't. The lizard didn't do anything."

"Oh Victoria, I wish I could have done something."

"It has nothing to do with you." Victoria looked her stepmother in the eye. "You weren't even in the picture then."

Iris nodded, her eyes filled with tears.

"Juan Carlos got into more trouble as a teenager," said her father to no one in particular. "But he turned out well in the end. He's an electrician now. Just got married, had a baby."

"Wasn't he accused of rape about two years ago?" Iris asked.

"He got off. Claimed it was consensual."

Miguel hurriedly interrupted to ask whether Victoria was feeling okay and remind her they really had to go. Andrés rose and took leave of Miguel, shaking hands warmly. Victoria stood up, but made no move to say goodbye. Iris held her close for a long moment. Andrés saw them to the door, urging them to come back soon, but he didn't accompany Iris to the car with the young couple.

Just as Miguel was starting the car, Iris remembered the pack of fruits and vegetables she had saved for them to take home. She rushed back into the house, and returned with a large bag. Her eyes moistening, she passed the fresh produce to Victoria.

Iris waved as the car disappeared down the driveway, and then walked back to the house and stood on the balcony for a long time. The late afternoon breeze felt cool on her cheeks wet with tears.

Fifteen minutes must have passed before Iris dried her face with her hand and went back inside. Andrés was sitting on the sofa. He handed her the used coffee cups to take to the kitchen and said, "You were silly to think they wouldn't come. The visit went pretty well, don't you think?"

Iris looked at him, not believing what she had just heard. "But Vicki seemed horribly upset about what happened with Juanky."

"Yeah, but what child doesn't have at least one run-in with a bully? It's part of the territory."

"Vicki seemed to think it was our fault."

"Couldn't have been your fault, mi amor. As she said, you weren't yet in the picture. The real point of the story was I'm the bad parent and her mother was the good parent who took her to the city. Of course, her mother just used the incident with Juanky as an excuse to leave."

"You never told me about Juanky."

"Mi amor, it wasn't such a big thing. My daughter is a drama queen like her mother."

"She was traumatized," said Iris.

The Pinch of the Crab

"Maybe you're right, mi amor. Childhood can be rough."

"The divorce must have been hard for her."

"Yeah, but she survived just fine. I like her husband. He's a good guy, don't you think?"

Iris nodded.

"Better than she deserves," said Andrés with a laugh that Iris didn't think quite succeeded in taking the sting out of the remark.

Victoria had not noticed the tears in her stepmother's eyes when she handed the bag of fruits and vegetables through the car window. Barely glancing at Iris, she took the bag, and murmured thank you. Miguel waved as they exited the driveway, but Victoria didn't turn around. She closed her eyes when they passed Don Cheo's house.

Once they reached the main road, Miguel patted her arm. "Now I understand why you weren't all that keen on visiting. Your father's a strange guy. The way he talked about your mother was unpardonable."

"He said a lot worse when she was alive."

"I really liked him at first. He seemed like such an intense guy, so passionate about growing things, preserving the natural habitat. But then he didn't react to what you were telling him. No affect. Went catatonic."

"That's the way he is."

"Your stepmother seemed genuinely upset. I couldn't help liking her."

"I used to like her, too."

"Used to?"

"Of course, at the beginning I resented her for taking my mother's place, but she's basically a good person, or would be if she weren't married to him."

"She doesn't have any children of her own?"

"No."

"Your father said she loved you like her own daughter."

En el campo

"When did my father come up with this talk about love?"

"While he was showing me the garden."

"What else did he say?"

"He said Iris cried for weeks after you left them to stay with your aunt."

So, her father hadn't wasted time to get Miguel on their side, tell him that his heartless daughter had left without a word. No wonder her father wasn't upset when she didn't go with them to the garden. He probably had it all planned with Iris. She showed me my bedroom with Blackie the bear still on my pillow while he worked on Miguel. And I'm supposed to feel guilty because my stepmother cried for three weeks. As though either of them cared about what happened to me.

"Pull over," she told Miguel.

Miguel pulled over as soon as there was enough shoulder to park the car safely. She got out, walked a little way down the road and knelt down to throw up the pollo criollo, gandules and flan. Miguel followed her, propped up her forehead with his hand, and went to get a thermos for her to rinse her mouth when she was done.

Victoria finally stood up and walked back to the car, but instead of getting in, she grabbed the bag of fresh produce. The bag was paper not plastic. Her father and stepmother were serious crusaders to save the planet. She hurled the entire contents on the ground, the grapefruits, cabbage and sweet peppers first, and then the tomatoes, one by one, taking pleasure as they splattered against the gravel. When there was nothing left to throw, she looked at the red pulp scattered around and repeated, "Goddamn crocodile tears," over and over again, until her husband persuaded her to get back in the car.

Once her sobs subsided, Miguel told her, "As far as I'm concerned, we don't have to go to Morovis ever again. It's not good for you to get so upset."

Iris had watched Miguel and Victoria's car disappear down the driveway, convinced she would never see her stepdaughter again. But as the weeks went by, she began to feel a jolt of hope each time the telephone rang. Time assuaged her perception of the visit as a disaster and made her receptive to her husband's more positive view. Telling the lizard story might have served as a catharsis for Victoria, a removal of old baggage to clear the path for a new adult relationship with her parents. After six weeks went by with no word, Iris told Andrés they should give a follow up call to see how the young couple was doing. Her husband said no way, the ball is in their park.

Iris waited a few days before bringing up the topic again. They had taken their customary early evening walk down the country road and back, and were seated on their front porch. The last tinges of pink in the sky were giving way to twilight, the approaching darkness alive with the sounds of coquis and crickets.

While they drank glasses of juice squeezed from their own oranges, Iris said, "Victoria put on weight, but it becomes her."

"Most women fill out in their twenties," agreed her husband. "Look over there, that dark cloud still has a rose lining."

Iris took a deep breath. Andrés had once told her that what bothered him most about the estrangement from his only daughter was that he would never see his grandchildren. "It crossed my mind that she might be pregnant."

Andrés withdrew his gaze from the heavens to look at his wife. "I didn't notice a belly."

"It wouldn't show at first."

Andrés shrugged. "Well, I'm sure you know more about it."

Iris decided to make her move. "That's why I really think we should call them again."

"Lo que tú quieras, mi amor. I trust your judgment."

Iris dialed Victoria's number when Andrés wasn't home. Miguel picked up the phone and spoke warmly about how much he had enjoyed meeting them. Victoria's voice was much colder when she came on the line, so frigid that Iris barely managed to stammer out an invitation to lunch. "Just the two of us."

En el campo

Victoria accepted and suggested they meet at La Patisserie in Plaza las Américas shopping mall. There's plenty of parking, now that they built the multistory lot on Roosevelt Avenue, she assured her stepmother.

Iris told her husband about the luncheon date. Andrés wanted to know who had invited whom. Iris surprised herself by telling a lie that it was Victoria's idea.

"And where are you ladies going?"

"La Patisserie at Plaza."

"No me sorprende. On her turf."

Iris arrived fifteen minutes early. After parking, she walked slowly, marveling at the remodeling and expansion of Plaza las Américas, advertised as the largest mall in the Caribbean. The restaurant was furnished in an eclectic modernistic style with glass and chrome mixed with wood and rustic tiles. She asked for a table for two, and sat down next to a large picture window facing a major corridor of the mall.

Iris had almost lost hope when Victoria appeared, elegantly dressed in heels, not too high, but enough to set off her long legs to advantage. She wore a loose-fitting blouse, but her pregnancy was unmistakable.

Once they had exchanged kisses, Iris exclaimed, "You know, I suspected you were pregnant when you came to the country, but I wasn't sure."

"The tests weren't conclusive yet," said Victoria.

"I can't believe my eyes. I'm so glad. Your father will be so excited when he hears."

The waitress came to take their order. A jumble of thoughts made it hard for Iris to concentrate on the menu. Had Victoria known and elected not to tell them? If she was telling the truth about not being sure, what prevented her from calling once the pregnancy was confirmed?

Iris asked Victoria to please order for her. They settled on crab salad and baguettes. To fill in a long silence, Iris asked which store would be best to look for a good shirt for Andrés. "Not too expensive, you know how your father dislikes extravagance." Victoria said both Penney's and Macy's have good sales.

The Pinch of the Crab

Iris turned the conversation back to her stepdaughter's pregnancy, asking for all the details including the due date. It wasn't until the waitress brought their coffees and chocolate éclairs that she ventured to touch upon what she had come to say.

"Victoria, I hope Miguel wasn't offended," she began, taking a sip of coffee. "I mean at our house."

"Why should Miguel be offended?"

"Your father said things... he shouldn't have."

Victoria put down the éclair and finished chewing, very properly with her mouth closed. Her expression was blank, as though a master ceramist had applied a hard glaze to make a portrait bust polished and impenetrable. "True, but what Papi said wasn't about Miguel was it?"

"No," Iris conceded.

"It was about Mami and about me."

Iris blinked back tears. "You're right. I'm making a mess of this. I'm sorry your father said those awful things. And I'm sorry if I did anything wrong. I'm not talking about when you and Miguel came to lunch. What I really want to know is what I did wrong before. Why did you run away to your aunt, never even saying goodbye?"

Victoria picked up a packet of sugar and stirred it into her coffee. "Miguel doesn't think I should talk about things that upset me while I'm pregnant."

"Of course, I just meant that I'd like to talk about it when you're ready."

"If we're going to talk, let's be honest. You know perfectly well why I left."

"Victoria, créeme, I don't know."

"Well, if you really don't, ask my father."

"Believe me. He is as mystified as I am," Iris replied, conscious of her stepdaughter's incredulous expression. "All your father told me is that love cannot be forced. If Victoria prefers to live with her mother's sister, that's her choice."

En el campo

"Goddamn bastard," said Victoria, her voice barely above a whisper. "Fucking liar."

Iris drew back. Her stepdaughter had never picked up the habit of easy swearing, which only made the words more caustic. She had to keep calm, and find out what was behind them.

"Vicki, does this have something to do with Juanky?"

"How did you guess?" replied her stepdaughter, a hint of mockery in her voice.

"It *is* just a guess," Iris protested.

"I didn't want to go over there for the birthday party, but your beloved husband made me go."

Iris remembered. Andrés had insisted that Victoria accompany them over to Don Cheo's place for his wife's birthday celebration. It became a battle royal when Victoria refused to go. Iris was puzzled, because her stepdaughter had always been fond of Doña Ines. Andrés accused her of thinking she was superior to country folk, betraying the jíbaro blood from which she came. Did she think that fancy hairdos and clothes make a lady? Doña Ines was more of a lady than Victoria would ever be. She had worked herself to the bone caring for seven kids and one stepson, and every single one was getting an education. Una dama genuina con un alma de oro. Victoria was yelled into submission. Her eyes still looked red when they walked over, but she kept her head up and greeted Doña Ines with a warm embrace.

"I knew Juanky would be there. Papi made me go and you did nothing."

"I didn't understand what was going on."

Victoria shrugged and adjusted her blouse over her full stomach. Iris recalled how she had been at sixteen, tall and willowy, with high fashion good looks, alabaster skin and dark eyes. Victoria had blushed scarlet when Doña Ines told her she had turned into a beautiful young lady.

Juan Carlos had looked handsome that night. He had become a man, tall and solidly built, with green eyes that were striking against his tawny skin. Andrés had teased him about the number of girls that must be after him. Iris had liked his answer. "Don Andrés, I'm looking not for any girl, but for that special one." Then he had gone outside where the younger crowd was hanging out. Victoria had lingered until Doña Ines told her to go on out, saying she must be bored indoors with the old folks.

"Papi knew what Juanky did to me when I was little," said Victoria.

"Did something happen that night?"

"Yeah. He asked me to dance. Just like that. Like the stones he'd thrown at me and the knife never existed. I said no. Then he said I was a stuck up blanquita. Accused me of thinking I was better than they were. What are you so stuck up, about? Look, fat Paco's got more boobs than you do. You're not even pretty."

Iris had received her share of teasing as a teenager for her chubby build and plain looks. It had never occurred to her that her stepdaughter, a beauty in her eyes, could have suffered the same adolescent angst.

"You seemed depressed when we got home," said Iris, "but I thought it was because of the fight with your father. Didn't he get annoyed with you again?"

"Yeah. You two were leaving for Santo Domingo for some conference the next morning, and he was angry because he thought I wasn't listening to his instructions about exactly how each plant was to be watered."

"The April drought had already begun."

Victoria shrugged. "Not that he would have been less insistent at some other time of year. Plants are more important than people."

In other circumstances, Iris would have protested that her stepdaughter's remark was unfair, but she kept quiet.

"He was wrong about me," said Victoria. "I took my responsibility to water and fertilize the plants very seriously."

Iris knew her stepdaughter was close to tears, if only because her voice was so carefully modulated to betray no emotion. The glaze that kept her face smooth and impenetrable did not crack. Iris reached out to touch her arm. "Miguel's right. You shouldn't get upset."

"I survived what happened, so I guess I'll survive talking about it."

En el campo

Iris wished she hadn't finished the crab salad. The restaurant might be chic, but the main ingredient of the sauce tasted like ordinary mayonnaise. No wonder it felt heavy on her stomach. Or maybe it was because after eight long years wondering what had gone wrong, she no longer wanted to know.

"You and my father left for the airport at dawn," said Victoria. "We had all gone to bed late the night before. You told me not to get up, you would lock the front door."

Iris nodded though she didn't remember.

"By the time I woke up," Victoria continued, "it was a hot day, deep blue sky with a couple of puffy clouds. Exactly the type of scorcher that would kill the young seedlings. My instructions were to wait until after five in the afternoon, when the sun was low in the sky. I unwound the long hose and started at the bottom, soaking each plant thoroughly, as I worked my way up the hill toward the house. The sun must have gone behind a cloud. While I was watering the newly planted citruses, I felt a sudden chill, you know a tingle at the nape of the neck, like a warning. I looked up. He was there, standing tall about ten feet above me, watching. Our house was behind him, silhouetted against the sky, the door wide open as I had left it."

Victoria stopped. There were no tears in her eyes, but between the strange choking sounds from her throat she got out the words, "I guess you know what happened next."

Iris got up and held her close, but Victoria disengaged herself.

"I called my aunt. It took me hours to work up the courage. I thought he would come back and kill me. Now you know."

Victoria wiped her eyes roughly with her napkin. Iris wanted to reach out and gently wipe away the smudge of mascara under one eye, but was afraid to touch her.

"I'm so sorry. It's my fault for being so stupid, so insensitive to what was going on. Dios mío, Don Cheo's brother took us to the airport."

"I guess that's how Juanky knew I would be alone."

The Pinch of the Crab

"Dime, Vicki, do you want me to tell your father?"

"He already knows."

"Are you sure?"

"My aunt told him. To let him know it was no use going to court to get me back. My aunt said she would counter sue for child neglect and reckless endangerment."

Iris sat very still. "This can't be true," she said. "He never told me. He lied to me. Oh my God. Your life was ruined, but I was blind, I didn't see, didn't suspect."

Victoria shrugged. "I got over it. My aunt took me to a psychiatrist. Then I joined a feminist group at the university. They were the ones that convinced me that it's still rape, even if you're too terrified to resist much. I'm okay."

"If the three of us are to have any future, be a family again, I have to tell your father what I know."

"I'm not sure I want a future," said Victoria.

"What do you mean?"

"What I said. Besides, you won't tell him."

"I have to."

"That's what you say now. But when you get home, you won't tell him that he lied to you. It would make him unhappy. You've always been the good wife. Not like that evil bitch."

"What bitch? What are you talking about?"

"My mother. Isn't that what he calls her?"

Iris didn't answer. She held Victoria's eyes for a brief moment before her stepdaughter looked away. Victoria paid the bill, rejecting her stepmother's protests that it was her treat. The next moment they were outside the restaurant, in the midst of a stream of shoppers. Victoria gave her a hasty peck on the cheek and said she had to go.

Iris clutched her arm and asked her to please call when the baby comes.

"If you like, I'll call *you*," said Victoria. "But I don't want my father at the hospital."

En el campo

Iris let go of her stepdaughter's arm. "I can't secretly visit you and the baby behind his back," she said, choking back tears.

"I'm sorry," said Victoria.

She leaned forward, kissed Iris on the cheek once more, and turned away, walking rapidly toward Macy's.

Iris stood and watched, sobbing openly now. Shoppers looked at her curiously. She stood still until Victoria took the escalator and disappeared into the store.

The drive home to Morovis seemed longer than usual. Andrés came out to greet his wife when she drove up the driveway. She told him Victoria was expecting.

"That's wonderful," said Andrés. "Does she know the sex yet?"

"It's a boy."

Andrés smiled. "I can just see him now. A little billy goat, jumping around the hills here on the farm."

Iris sighed. "That's the good news. The bad news is that Vicki doesn't want us in her life."

"She made you go all the way to San Juan to tell you that? What a little bitch. Just like her mother."

Iris said nothing.

Andrés turned on his heel and went back into the house. Iris lingered a while outside, picturing Victoria watering the lemon tree, ten yards below the house. It had been a small sapling, recently planted, a couple of feet high. In eight years, it had become a full grown tree, its main trunk bent over to the ground by hurricane Georges.

She walked down and stood next to the tree, facing the house. A man stared down at her, his feet planted apart, his biceps bulging under his T-shirt, positioned midway between her and the open door. She screamed no, no, no, her hands clutching her head, pulling at the roots of her hair, but the film reel inside her head wouldn't stop until she curled her hand around a branch of the lemon tree, pressing down while the spines bored into her skin and the blood flowed.

The Pinch of the Crab

When she got inside the house, she ran cold water over the cuts, applied a disinfectant, and put on a bandage. Andrés didn't emerge from his study until she called him for supper. He didn't comment on her bandaged hand. After they had eaten in silence, he said, "Amor, don't be sad. You did your best. There's nothing more we can do. Children grow up different from what you expect. Believe me, being with you here on our farm is enough for me—it always has been and always will be."

Iris nodded, not trusting herself to answer. Her husband went to bed as usual at nine o'clock to get an early morning start. When he called her to come to bed, she pleaded a headache. She would have to stay up until the two Tylenols kicked in.

Iris picked up a magazine from the coffee table, but the words made no sense to her. She walked to the hallway and paused in the doorway of the bedroom, listening to her husband's steady snore. Then she turned away and tiptoed into the room that had once been her stepdaughter's. Blackie the Bear was still lying between the two pillows, but his fur no longer smelled of Victoria.

Appendices

Acknowledgements

The author would like to express a debt of profound gratitude to María Soledad Rodríguez, Yolanda Rivera Castillo and Elena Torruella, three writers of prose and poetry, who read and reread various versions of these stories with a critical but benevolent eye, praising strong points and patiently pointing out weaknesses of plot, structure and wording. Their supportive critiques were invaluable to my development as a writer. Needless to say, any fault in the final product is my own.

I would also like to thank my former colleagues and dear friends María de los Ángeles Castro, Gervasio García, María Dolores Luque, Carlos Ramos and Carol Romey for their suggestions and encouragement. My family has also been very supportive. My husband, Parimal Choudhury, has been a perceptive critic, faithfully pointing out passages that were unclear or might be misinterpreted. My daughter, Shonali Choudhury, made valuable suggestions, particularly regarding point of view in the last story in this collection. My son, Shubin Choudhury, checked to see whether popular lingo was accurately depicted in stories like "Strike Three." Many thanks to my twelve-year-old granddaughter, Shaila Choudhury Madero, for the painting depicting a crab on the beach and her help designing the cover of the book.

Lastly, I would like to thank my students at the University of Puerto Rico for not only sharing with me their intellectual interests, but also their insights into the workings of the society and culture that shaped their formative years.

About the Author

Barbara Southard has been writing short stories and historical novels since retiring from the University of Puerto Rico at Río Piedras. In addition to teaching US and Asian history, she served as Chairperson of the History Department and Associate Dean of Graduate Studies. She published a book on the women's movement in India in the nineteen twenties and thirties, and co-authored with Mayra Rosario two text books for high school students on the history of the United States. Her short stories have been published in *Poui: Cave Hill Journal of Creative Writing, Calabash, The Journal of Caribbean Literatures,* and *Cerebrations.* She is a founding member of the online literary journal *Moonwired: Literary Review of the Women Writers' Bilingual Collective of Puerto Rico/Amanecidas: Revista literaria de la colectiva bilingüe de escritoras de Puerto Rico* (www.moonwired.org). The memoir she submitted to the annual contest held by Kore press, *Uneven Cobblestones: Walking with My Daughter on Her Last Journey* was selected as a semi-finalist. At present, she is working on revising a historical novel and raising funds for the Shonali Choudhury Fund (honoring her daughter who died of a brain tumor) of the Fundación Comunitaria de Puerto Rico to help community organizations working to protect women from domestic violence.

Reseña (Book Review)
The Pinch of the Crab and other stories
Carmen Dolores Hernández: El Nuevo Día, 13 de febrero de 2022

El libro de las traiciones

Una mujer casada revive un incidente terrible de su juventud que sus padres han elegido ignorar; una joven descubre la verdadera personalidad del padre que la crió con cariño; un niño pequeño se enfrenta a la violencia -de los animales, del entorno social y la que irrumpe en la familia -sin entender bien lo que sucede; unos padres culpan a un amigo de su hijo por "corromperlo" cuando lo cierto es justamente lo contrario.

Los diez cuentos de este libro giran todos en torno a traiciones. Son traiciones especialmente dolorosas que se dan en el seno de familias que parecen ser, si no felices, más o menos normales. Lo que provoca el conflicto es un cambio de perspectiva ocasionado por una falla de las expectativas habituales: los padres que no son, realmente, protectores; las madres que no resultan tan dedicadas; el amargo descubrimiento de que el amor no es tan duradero ni tan absoluto como lo esperado. La falla -la grieta en

The Pinch of the Crab

la superficie pulida de las expectativas convencionales- ha estado allí desde el principio, invisible para los ojos confiados.

El cuento titulado "Heavy Downpour" se aparta un poco de este esquema. En él no es la familia ni uno de sus miembros lo que traiciona las expectativas de justicia sino la sociedad misma, que persigue a quien trata de practicar esa justicia, trastocando al hacerlo el orden establecido. El personaje que aparece en casa de una próspera ama de casa estadounidense radicada en Puerto Rico, un amigo de su juventud rebelde, parece presentar una amenaza, tanto para ella como para la colectividad, pero esa percepción está equivocada. El peligro real proviene de la sociedad establecida, que no provee las salvaguardas adecuadas para la vida y el progreso social. Es la estructura política la que traiciona las expectativas de equidad, justicia y democracia. El asunto se refiere a la situación política puertorriqueña, aparentemente estable, aunque cualquier amenaza a tal estabilidad suscite la violencia institucional.

Barbara Southard, estadounidense que lleva muchos años en Puerto Rico, los más como profesora de la UPR, ha sabido penetrar tras el espejismo de las apariencias no solo individuales sino sociales. Sus cuentos, más que críticos, son revelatorios. El ambiente local -muy bien captado- presenta un espejo de la naturaleza humana en su modalidad puertorriqueña: la incapacidad de enfrentarse a la realidad, la necesidad de mantener las apariencias, las convenciones relativas a la familia. Son actitudes difícilmente discernibles para quienes están inmersos en la sociedad que las sustenta, pero quizás evidentes ante la mirada de afuera. La nuestra es una sociedad que se cree estable aunque la violencia -súbita, inesperada- se esconda tras las convenciones generalmente aceptadas.

Southard escribe en un inglés directo y sencillo. Su estilo no llama la atención sobre sí; se trata más bien de un filtro que permite "leer" no solo los significados de las palabras sino las intenciones que se esconden tras ellas y que no son inmediatamente aparentes a los interlocutores de dentro de los cuentos mismos. Maneja bien, además, las premoniciones y también las sorpresas, como en el cuento "Fallen Branches", cuya acción parece apuntar en una dirección para culminar con un estallido inesperado.

Aunque Southard ha escrito varios libros de carácter histórico, entre ellos "Senderos para un sueño. Geografía e historia de Estados Unidos de América" (2000), con este volumen de cuentos se suma a la ya larga lista de escritores estadounidenses de ficción que han utilizado a Puerto Rico como escenario o motivación para su escritura, lista que incluye a Hunter S. Thompson y a Robert Friedman.

www.ingramcontent.com/pod-product-compliance
Lightning Source LLC
Chambersburg PA
CBHW031148020426
42333CB00013B/566